In an era when so many ministers are skillfully avoiding "hot button" issues and concentrating on improving the church's image in the world, I really appreciate how *Unleashed* calls for the church to boldly take a stand for truth and holiness. This is outstanding!

—Bob Russell, retired senior minister of
Southeast Christian Church, Louisville, KY

Through an insightful and powerful look at the church—in the first century and now—*Unleashed* challenges Christians to boldly live out God's design for their lives.

—Miles McPherson, former NFL player,
senior pastor of the Rock Church, San Diego, CA

I can't imagine a more timely book, a more urgent subject matter, and a more inspiring team of authors. Thank you for calling us to break loose and serve with new courage, pray bolder prayers, and trust God for supernatural results.

—Gene Appel, senior pastor of
Eastside Christian Church, Fullerton, CA

Knowing the burden my friend Dudley Rutherford has for reaching the entire world for Christ, I am thrilled that he and other fabulous pastors have written *Unleashed*. This is a must-read for those who study the early church in the book of Acts and long for today's church to possess that same dynamism and effectiveness. Read it. You will never be the same!

—]
Skyline W

D0924065

If you prefer the status quo, this book is not for you. If you like your Christianity tame, domesticated, and risk free, you won't like this book. But if you are eager to see a Spirit-inspired revival sweep through the church—beginning with you—then read on. And prepare to be *Unleashed!*

—Rick Atchley, minister of the Word,
The Hills Church of Christ, Richland Hills, TX

unleashed

unleashed

the church

turning the world

upside down

Dudley Rutherford | Daryl Reed | Greg Nettle | Francis Chan
Phil Allen | Dave Stone | Jeff Walling | Mike Breaux | Jeff Vines

Standard® PUBLISHING

Cincinnati, Ohio

Published by Standard Publishing, Cincinnati, Ohio
www.standardpub.com

Copyright © 2011 by Standard Publishing

Printed in: United States of America
Editor: Dale Reeves
Cover design: Scott Ryan
Interior design: Andrew Quach

ISBN 978-0-7847-3179-6

Unleashed : the church turning the world upside down / Dudley Rutherford ... [et al.].
    p. cm.
  Includes bibliographical references (p.   ).
  ISBN 978-0-7847-3179-6 (perfect bound with hinge score)
  1. Church--Biblical teaching. 2. Bible. N.T. Acts--Criticism, interpretation, etc. I. Rutherford, Dudley.
  BS2625.6.C5U55 2011
  226.6'06--dc22
                        2011006862

16 15 14 13 12 11   1 2 3 4 5 6 7 8 9

| Acknowledgments |

What an indescribable joy it has been to see my passion and vision for this book realized, knowing it would not have been possible without the help of some wonderful people whom I love and respect immensely.

First, I must thank the leadership of the 2011 North American Christian Convention, who agreed to allow me to do this project. Having a book accompany the NACC is something that had never been done before, and I appreciate the board of stewards, managing director Larry Collins, and his staff for believing in me, for being a great source of encouragement along the way, and for their hard work in organizing the convention.

I also want to thank Dale Reeves at Standard Publishing for his great enthusiasm and diligence in coordinating the many moving pieces to make this book a reality. Dale, thank you so much for championing this project.

I am so very humbled by and thankful for the gracious participation of Daryl Reed, Greg Nettle, Mike Breaux, Phil Allen, Dave Stone, Jeff Vines, Francis Chan, and Jeff Walling—both in this book and in the 2011 NACC. I admire each of you for your commitment to partner with the Holy Spirit's work here on earth and for the incredible things you are doing within your ministries. Thank you for taking time out of your busy schedules to join with me on this project.

I would be remiss not to thank my assistant, Angie Merrill, and the assistants of the other eight authors. Your faithful work behind the scenes has kept us on target for meeting our deadlines. As *Unleashed* influences believers to change the world for Christ, please know that each of you is a part of that.

I want to thank my beautiful wife, Renee, and our children for the time they allowed me not only to produce this book but to plan the NACC for the last two years. Thank you for your love and sacrifice, which enable me to pursue that which God has placed on my heart.

Finally, I feel compelled to thank Don DeWelt, one of my professors at Ozark Christian College. His in-depth teaching on the book of Acts and the work of the Holy Spirit shaped my life and my ministry—and I am eternally grateful.

—Dudley Rutherford

Contents

unleashed

Acts 1:1-8; 17:6

I n an elegant meeting room in West Los Angeles, I sat with five other pastors from Southern California when *he* walked in. Arnold Schwarzenegger. Yes, *that* Arnold Schwarzenegger. The champion bodybuilder, movie star, husband to Maria Shriver of the Kennedy dynasty, businessman, and then governor of the state of California.

He greeted each of us warmly and took a seat immediately to my right. Suddenly, I was shoulder to shoulder with this man who was indeed larger than life. He was like a Greek god—tall, tan, with gleaming white teeth, and in superior shape for a man in his early sixties. At that time, Schwarzenegger governed the most populous and third largest state in the union, with close to thirty-seven million people,[1] which is approximately one-eighth the population of the entire United States.[2]

The five other pastors and I were there to confront him, *mano a mano,* about his support of same-sex marriage and his opposition to Proposition 8, which had just passed in our state. As you may recall, Prop 8 is an amendment to the California State Constitution, providing that "only marriage between a man and a woman is valid or recognized in California."[3] It sparked a heated, nationwide debate.

What am I doing here? I pondered during this very surreal moment in time. *I thought I was called to win people to Jesus, to visit the sick in hospitals and the elderly in nursing homes, to disciple others and draw them closer to Jesus. What am I, a pastor of a church, doing confronting a political figure, who—if it weren't for the fact that he's disqualified because he wasn't born in the United States—would probably not only run for president but stand a good chance of actually winning?*

The Cultural Tsunami

I was here because, in California where I live and pastor, the culture war between the church and the world is at an all-time high. We see it in Hollywood and in the entertainment industry. It's visible in the liberal, left-wing politics, and the fact that our San Fernando Valley is the number one producer of pornography in the world. The West Coast is not a conservative area, unlike the Bible Belt and midwestern America. Here, our church is positioned as a light in the midst of a truly dark place where morals are mocked, values are vilified, and righteousness is ridiculed.

> The culture war between the church and the world is at an all-time high.

My view of ministry in the church has been simply to preach the gospel, serve the kingdom of God, lift up Jesus, and see the world come to him. But in the process of building our church and striving to be a light in the community, I realized one day that we had been conducting ministry primarily *inside* our four walls. Sure, we ventured out from time to time for service projects such as food drives for the homeless, clothing collection for the needy, blankets for the elderly, and backpacks for school children—which are all worthy causes. But while I continued to pastor and minister in a typical fashion, I had come to see that the world was changing around us. The tide was turning. I started to feel more and more every day as though I was being deluged by a cultural tsunami . . . as though we, the church, were losing the battle of the church influencing the world for Christ vs. the world influencing the church.

I could not believe that in the United States of America we would even be having a discussion, let alone a debate, about how marriage should be defined. After Proposition 8 was placed on the ballot, it dawned on us as California pastors that if we didn't get involved, if we didn't stand up for righteousness and let our voices be heard, same-sex marriage would soon be the norm.

And thus it began. As if in a riptide, I got pulled into a political process in which I never imagined being involved. Never in my wildest dreams did I think we'd be fighting to defend and uphold the historical and biblical definition of marriage. In leading my own church in the fight, I felt like I was fighting for all the churches in America. I felt like I was standing on the precipice of our nation's future, and I was reminded of a stirring passage in Ezekiel that appears immediately after God expresses his indignation toward the wickedness, injustice, and oppression that had become so prevalent in the land of Israel at the

> I got pulled into a political process in which I never imagined being involved.

time: "I looked for someone among them who would build up the wall and stand before me in the gap on behalf of the land so I would not have to destroy it, but I found no one. So I will pour out my wrath on them and consume them with my fiery anger, bringing down on their own heads all they have done, declares the Sovereign LORD" (Ezekiel 22:30, 31).

Does that passage make you shudder? Does it burden your heart for our nation as it burdens mine? It should, for it is a sobering reminder to Christians everywhere of the dire consequences that will result if we don't stand "in the gap" on behalf of our country.

With the battle lines drawn in regard to the Prop 8 debate, my fellow pastors and I had to decide whether or not we were going to take a stand for God and marriage in our nation, or allow America to get swept away like other great nations that have been cut down by sin and indifference. United as one, we had no choice but to take a stand.

unleashed

All of a sudden, attacks began from both inside and outside the church, from believers in Jesus and nonbelievers alike, arguing that we should not be engaged in social wars like same-sex marriage and abortion. Yet I felt that if we didn't get involved, all of America would continue to drift to a place beyond repair.

In the midst of the kind of extreme tension that results when the church and the world are in direct conflict with one another, I knew I needed biblical guidance to navigate these rough waters.

A Dynamite Promise

With laser-like focus, I dug deep into God's Word in an effort to rediscover the foundational pillars and paradigms of the church in the first century. I was desperately trying to determine whether there was biblical precedent for Christians to wade into the culture wars and for pastors to engage in these issues in their preaching and priorities. Naturally, I began my journey in the book of Acts, which documents the inception of the early church—and what I found was nothing short of astonishing.

> I dug deep into God's Word in an effort to rediscover the foundational pillars and paradigms of the church in the first century.

Before ascending to Heaven, Jesus promised his apostles that if they waited prayerfully and patiently in Jerusalem, God would give them the gift of the Holy Spirit (Acts 1:4, 5). That promise was fulfilled in Acts 2 in a supernatural way that took place on the Day of Pentecost— the miraculous moment in which God imparted his Spirit to the early Christians with mighty signs and wonders, filling faithful believers and leaving onlookers "utterly amazed" (vv. 2-12).

What was so special about this unleashing of the Spirit of God? It wasn't simply a spectacle of speaking in tongues, rushing wind, and flames of fire (vv. 2-4). Earlier, in Luke 24:45-49, Jesus had actually explained to his followers that they would be "clothed with power from on high." In Acts 1:8, he expounded further: "You will receive power when the Holy Spirit comes on you; and you will be my witnesses in Jerusalem, and in all Judea and Samaria, and to the ends of the earth." So we see that the main benefit of this gift of the Holy Spirit was witness-enabling, God-glorifying, supernatural power for Christ's church!

The Greek word for "power" is *dunamis,* from which we get the word *dynamite.*[4] The Scriptures tell us that God has placed dynamite, *dunamis* power, within each and every follower of Jesus—no matter our position, size, economic status, race, gender, or age.

> God has placed dynamite, *dunamis* power, within each and every follower of Jesus.

Because I'm a sports aficionado and a father, I've often helped as an assistant coach for the boys' and girls' high school basketball teams at the Christian academy affiliated with our church. The girls' head coach, Debbie Haliday, teaches not only the x's and o's of the game of basketball, but she's also a highly gifted spiritual mentor. Every year she selects a biblical theme for the team for the entire season. When my oldest daughter was a freshman playing on the team, Coach Haliday chose the theme *dunamis.* Their theme verse was Ephesians 3:20: "Now to him who is able to do immeasurably more than all we ask or imagine, according to his *power* that is at work within us . . ." (emphasis added).

Uniquely, Coach Haliday had the word *dunamis* printed on the backs of all the warm-up uniforms, instead of the players' last names that typically would be displayed. So while the girls warmed up before the games in their new jerseys, players from the other teams would ask them about the word *dunamis.* Imagine these high school girls explaining on a regular basis that *dunamis* means "power" in the original Greek. Whenever I was asked by an opponent or by someone sitting in the stands, I always replied that *dunamis* is a Greek word that means "We do not miss!"

All kidding aside, this led to many great conversations among the players about God giving us a power that is greater than our own through his wonderful, supernatural Spirit.

Power Displayed

While Acts 2 details how God's Spirit was unleashed upon the church, the rest of the *entire* book of Acts chronicles the church being unleashed upon the world. In almost every chapter, we see *dunamis* power demonstrated in the first-century Christians in a remarkable fashion—both individually and corporately—and impacting the culture around them. Here are just a few examples of what we observe:

- a beggar being healed, though he had been disabled since birth (Acts 3:7-10)
- ordinary, unschooled disciples preaching with a courage that astounded and befuddled those in authority (Acts 4:13)
- countless people being healed and becoming believers, all as a result of the signs and wonders performed by the apostles (Acts 5:12-16)
- a man named Stephen witnessing with boldness and, later, dying willingly at the hands of his persecutors for his faith and belief in the Lord Jesus Christ (Acts 7)
- an Ethiopian official believing the gospel and getting baptized (Acts 8:26-39)
- a vehement persecutor of the church suddenly becoming a believer (Acts 9:1-16)
- a disciple being miraculously released from prison (Acts 12:5-11)
- a jailer, who had been overseeing Paul and Silas in prison, accepting the gift of salvation after a violent earthquake (Acts 16:25-34)

The early church became a mighty, energetic, conspicuous, eye-opening movement. It went from being a footnote to being a headline on the front page of every newspaper. With great influence and potency, the early church confronted the world, bucked the status quo, and stood against the ever-changing tide of culture.

The human traditions of the religious and political leaders were threatened, so they persecuted Jesus' followers—arresting, imprisoning, flogging, and ordering them to stop preaching in the name of Jesus. And by the time we get to Acts 17:6, the church in the first century was actually accused of turning the whole world "upside down" *(NKJV)*.

> The early church confronted the world, bucked the status quo, and stood against the ever-changing tide of culture.

Can you imagine such a thing? It was this power and anointing of the Holy Spirit that transformed a team of ragtag, uneducated Galileans into a lean, mean, fighting machine—a group of followers who took the world by storm.

Status Quo or Spirit Flow?

In studying the Word of God, the example set by those courageous New Testament heroes, and the change they inspired throughout the world, I stood back and looked at the modern-day church and arrived at a most troubling conclusion: the church in America *barely* reflects the church in the book of Acts. Before you tune me out, please allow me to explain.

There are many churches today that neglect, misunderstand, or fail to seize the *dunamis* power from the Holy Spirit that is supernaturally available to us as Christians. Don't get me wrong; there are many wonderful examples in our fellowship of churches right now. At last fall's National Missionary Convention, I observed thousands of young

unleashed

people who have dedicated themselves to worldwide mission projects. Bible colleges are working together like never before in their effort to educate and equip young believers from diverse backgrounds for ministry. Organizations like the Exponential Network, Stadia, and Orchard Group are planting churches across America and throughout the world. We have seen a resurgence of the North American Christian Convention and Youth for Christ. There is the megachurch phenomenon in which droves of people are coming to hear the message of the cross. Churches both large and small, in remote as well as densely populated areas, are seeing lives being changed and victories in social justice issues every single day.

> We have seen a continual erosion of the vigor, strength, and influence in the church.

But the bottom line is, there are more than three hundred million people living in America today,[5] and the vast majority of them do not know Jesus Christ. The church has been successful throughout different sections of the country, but we have yet to see a revival on a large-scale basis that sweeps across the land; we have yet to see a cultural shift toward righteousness and holiness. When you look at:

- the ongoing proliferation of the use of pornography, a $13 billion dollar industry[6]
- the escalating divorce rate over the past several decades[7]
- the fact that close to fifty million abortions have occurred in the United States since Roe v. Wade in 1973[8]
- the growing acceptance and approval of same-sex marriage
- the lack of Christian witness on our university campuses
- the fact that Las Vegas, aka Sin City, remains one of the top ten vacation destinations in the U.S.[9]

- the number of people who are unsaved, unchurched, and without a relationship with Jesus Christ
- the number of churches that have become stagnant and dormant in their growth and effectiveness . . .

. . . it becomes overwhelmingly obvious that we still have a very long way to go in order to accurately mirror the church of the New Testament.

This is perhaps most evident here on the West Coast, where we have seen a continual erosion of the vigor, strength, and influence in the church. Within a ten-year period of time—from 1990 to 2000—the number of churches in our fellowship in California fell from three hundred to two hundred.[10] Literally one-third of our churches closed their doors. They locked up the building, closed shop, and seemed to have run for the hills.

> The church needs to be inquisitive about its lack of vitality in today's world.

What happened? Where did the power go? Why have so many churches shut their doors? How are we failing? Why are so many churches all across America hurting and becoming overwhelmed by this cultural tsunami? These are honest questions that deserve our time and attention. Just as a patient desires a trustworthy diagnosis of his or her illness, the church needs to be inquisitive about its lack of vitality in today's world.

There could be a number of reasons why the church seems to be losing the culture war. It could be:

- sin—that we as a nation have drifted so far away from God that he simply has removed his hand of blessing.
- financial difficulty hampering our evangelistic endeavors—because money has become the god of many, and even those within the church

unleashed

refuse to bring the whole tithe into God's house (Malachi 3:9-11).

- division, for a house divided cannot stand—and yet there are so many doctrinal and denominational chasms within the church today.

- the inability to overcome opposition or discouragement, or a fear of allowing God's Spirit to lead—hindering the flowing power and joy that could amaze those around us.

- that some of our church leaders are unsaved—because the Bible makes it very clear that the Holy Spirit of God indwells those who are saved, and that means we should have *power*.

- biblical illiteracy contributing to a mingling of New Age spirituality with Christianity—happening even in quite conservative churches—and rendering church leaders and members ill equipped for battle.

For whatever reason, we often find ourselves in a defensive posture as Christians. If this were a football game, our backs would be against the goal line with our opponent positioned to score the winning touchdown. The church needs to intercept the ball, get back on the offensive, be aggressive, and regain momentum. We must begin to advance and impact every segment of society in order to win this cultural battle.

> It was God's plan all along for the church to be on the offensive.

When we look at Christ's departing words in Matthew 28:18-20, it becomes clear that it was God's plan all along for the church to be on the offensive—in our evangelistic fervor, in our quest to make disciples of all nations, in our utilization of the resurrection power of Jesus, and in our obedience to the Great Commission. There, in his final instructions to the church, the Lord chose an *active* word, "go." And he promised that his church would be so victorious that even "the powers of hell will not conquer it" (Matthew 16:18, *NLT*). This promise should catalyze the church to march triumphantly; move forward; experience success; gain ground; and influence the culture, media, entertainment, local and national governments . . . and even the PTA in our neighborhood schools.

Church on Steroids

If the apostle Paul were alive today, certainly he would urge the church to rejoice in the fact that we are victorious and powerful in Christ Jesus. Can someone say "Amen!" One of the most unequivocal proofs of this is found in Romans 16:25-27, in which Paul writes: "Now to him who is able to establish you in accordance with my gospel, the message I proclaim about Jesus Christ, in keeping with the revelation of the mystery hidden for long ages past, but now revealed and made known through the prophetic writings by the command of the eternal God, so that all the Gentiles might come to the obedience that comes from faith—to the only wise God be glory forever through Jesus Christ! Amen."

Paul asserts that God is able to "establish" you and me. The word *establish* comes from the Greek word *sterizo*,[11] from which we get the word *steroids*.

> While steroids give athletes an unfair advantage, the church also has an advantage—except that it's not illegal or unfair.

We hear a lot about anabolic steroids in the sports world today, because some athletes have been caught using them to enhance their performance. While steroids give athletes an unfair advantage, the church also has an advantage—except that it's not illegal or unfair, because the power of God is available to everyone who believes. That passage from Romans reveals that God has given Christians *sterizo*-like power so all nations would be reached (v. 26) and so God would be glorified (v. 27)!

Therefore, believers ultimately will have victory because God is on our side. However, he's much more than *on* our side or even *by* our side—

unleashed

he's actually *inside,* for his Spirit dwells within us. Because of this truth, the church is a Holy Spirit–enabled force to be reckoned with, and we have all the necessary tools to succeed. May we, as Christians, open our hearts fully to the guidance and power of the Holy Spirit, to move from status quo to Spirit flow, and pray that the Spirit will *sterizo* (establish) us like never before!

Disruption and Political Upheaval

But be forewarned. With this power, you will undoubtedly cause quite a commotion wherever you go, just as Christ and his first-century followers did. Whenever Jesus or his disciples rolled into town with such unstoppable momentum, the political and religious systems were confronted by the power of God being displayed in the midst of ordinary people. Those in authority did the only thing they could do, for fear of losing their standing in the community: they turned against the early disciples by threatening, imprisoning, flogging, and persecuting them. The authorities would do anything to silence this group belonging to "the Way" (Acts 9:2), attempting to stifle their voice and influence so they themselves could maintain control and power over the people.

Multiple threats and emphatic demands not to speak or teach in the name of Jesus were an attempt to scare Christians into being silent. Oftentimes those fear tactics worked. They still work today.

It is my belief that the modern-day church would love to stand up and speak out on the abortion issue, but many of us won't because we're afraid we're going to offend others, lose members, or be persecuted as a result. We would love to stand up and preach that marriage is a union between a man and a woman, but we're afraid we're going to upset people sitting in our congregations—who are either homosexual or sympathetic to the homosexual agenda—and then be attacked or criticized. But we need to understand that whenever we are "speaking the truth in love" (Ephesians 4:15), whenever we lift high the name of Jesus (John 3:14), whenever we let our lights shine (Matthew 5:16) or stand for the rights of the unborn child (see Proverbs 31:8), we will always face persecution and criticism from those who wish to silence the righteousness and holiness of Jesus Christ.

Sometimes we forget that Jesus himself offended his fellow citizens, religious and political leaders, and even his own disciples at times (Matthew 13:53-58; 15:12; Mark 6:3; Luke 7:23; John 6:61). Certainly I don't think any of us should set a goal to see how many people we can

> Sometimes we forget that Jesus himself offended his fellow citizens, religious and political leaders, and even his own disciples at times.

offend. But as Christians we do aspire to hold high the name of Jesus, and in the process of lifting up Jesus, we will inevitably offend others.

We are called to be like Jesus and to preach like Jesus, in an unadulterated way. But in order to do this, the church must accept *everything* about Christ as described in the Word of God—*all* the facets of his marvelous character, even the ones that are difficult to embrace. Here are three aspects about our Lord, the chief cornerstone of the church, that you may never have considered before.

1. Consider Jesus' Winnowing Fork

Our very first view of Jesus in the Gospels was provided by John the Baptist, the forerunner to the Messiah. He conveyed a well-known description of Jesus Christ when he stated in Matthew 3:11, "I baptize you with water for repentance. But after me comes one who is more powerful than I, whose sandals I am not worthy to carry. He will baptize you with the Holy Spirit and fire."

unleashed

You may be familiar with those words, but in the church we have not emphasized verse 12, in which John the Baptist indicated what Jesus was going to do upon his arrival: "His winnowing fork is in his hand, and he will clear his threshing floor, gathering his wheat into the barn and burning up the chaff with unquenchable fire."

What does *that* mean? His "winnowing fork"? "Gathering his wheat into the barn and burning up the chaff"? Whoa. That's not what most of us think about when we think about Jesus. But *that's* Jesus. The Word of God says that Christ is going to purge, purify, and separate out that which is fruitful from that which is fruitless. It's not very comfortable to think about, but that's Jesus—and we must not hold back from this truth in our bold witness to save as many people as possible from the "unquenchable fire."

2. Consider What Jesus Actually Preached

Matthew 4:17 says, "From that time on Jesus began to preach, 'Repent, for the kingdom of heaven has come near.'" Jesus preached *repentance.* Many of us share the love of Christ—his awesome mercy and grace toward each of us—but in our desire not to offend, sometimes we omit the truth that Christ preached repentance from sins.

> In our desire not to offend, sometimes we omit the truth that Christ preached repentance from sins.

Whenever we preach against any kind of sin, it will result in a certain rejection from the world, because people desire to remain in their sin and will, therefore, attempt to discredit, dissuade, and derail the messenger of truth. As Christians we must accept that this is inevitable—Jesus told us this very thing more than two thousand years ago: "I have told you these things, so that in me you may have peace. In this world you will have trouble. But take heart! I have overcome the world" (John 16:33).

We must stay faithful to our duty to preach as Jesus preached by telling others about the necessity of repentance, for the kingdom of Heaven is near. We must *expect* opposition, troubles, and rejection as a result of sharing our faith—and we must face these trials with courage.

3. Consider Jesus' Prediction of Persecution

When Jesus sent out the twelve disciples on his behalf in Matthew 10:7, 8, he challenged them: "As you go, proclaim this message: 'The kingdom of heaven has come near.' Heal the sick, raise the dead, cleanse those who have leprosy, drive out demons. Freely you have received; freely give." And then he issued this stern warning and prophetic instruction: "Be on your guard; you will be handed over to the local councils and be flogged in the synagogues. On my account you will be brought before governors and kings as witnesses to them and to the Gentiles. But when they arrest you, do not worry about what to say or how to say it. At that time you will be given what to say" (vv. 17-19).

Jesus did not use words such as *might* and *if* in the above passage, but *will* and *when*. It's inescapable—persecution is promised to those who faithfully proclaim his message. The old, rugged cross at Calvary, upon which our Savior was crucified, is the ultimate example of what happens when we stand for the truth and turn the world upside down in the name of God's one and only Son, Jesus Christ. When we gaze at that cross, it should serve not only as a reminder of God's great love and sacrifice for us (John 3:16; Romans 5:8) but also as an assurance that if we are truly living and preaching as Jesus did, many of us will face fierce persecution and even death for sake of the gospel.

Though this may worry or scare some, remember that "God has not given us a spirit of fear, but of power and of love and of a sound mind" (2 Timothy 1:7, *NKJV*).

unleashed

Reality Check

The early church embraced with complete abandon those examples from Jesus' life and teaching. They preached the fullness of the gospel and stood courageously before the world, regardless of violating politically correct jargon or fearing an onslaught of persecution. But do we?

How many of us have gone to prison for the sake of the gospel or have been dragged before governors and kings to be a witness to them of God's saving grace through Jesus Christ? How many of us have endured threats or beatings or intense ridicule for preaching the Word? Yet 2 Timothy 3:12 says, "Everyone who wants to live a godly life in Christ Jesus will be persecuted." The biblical precedent shows us that Christians in high positions and low positions, and everyone in between, need to flavor and penetrate the culture with courage and conviction. Tom Minnery, in his book *Why You Can't Stay Silent*, writes:

> "Everyone who wants to live a godly life in Christ Jesus will be persecuted."

Today's society is decaying, and the darkness of secular life grows. In circumstances like these, the witness of Christians should be noticeable, and it is quite natural at times that it will be controversial. If it is not—if Christians are coasting along in perfect contentment with the state of things or are blissfully ignorant of current events—then Christ's powerful metaphors of salt and light mean nothing to them. They miss the full scope of what it means to be Christian. This is particularly true in an era like our own, when the preserving chemistry of salt and the illumination of divine light are so desperately needed. . . . Being salt and light in this age means contending responsibly for godly standards wherever they are under assault.[12]

The essence of our calling to be the salt and light of the world (Matthew 5:13-16) is to impact the culture in which we live—*not* to allow the culture to impact the church. In the great battle that is being waged this very moment, the consequences of inactivity, indifference, fear, or failure are too costly to ignore.

A Train in the Distance

In his book *When a Nation Forgets God,* Erwin Lutzer gives this haunting, eyewitness account of how a particular church reacted to the Nazism of the times:

> I lived in Germany during the Nazi Holocaust. I considered myself a Christian. We heard stories of what was happening to the Jews, but we tried to distance ourselves from it, because, what could anyone do to stop it?
>
> A railroad track ran behind our small church and each Sunday morning we could hear the whistle in the distance and then the wheels coming over the tracks. We became disturbed when we heard the cries coming from the train as it passed by. We realized that it was carrying Jews like cattle in the cars!
>
> Week after week the whistle would blow. We dreaded to hear the sound of those wheels because we knew that we would hear the cries of the Jews en route to a death camp. Their screams tormented us.
>
> We knew the time the train was coming and when we heard the whistle blow we began singing hymns. By the time the train came past our church we were singing at the top of our voices. If we heard the screams, we sang more loudly and soon we heard them no more.

unleashed

> Years have passed and no one talks about it anymore.
> But still I hear that train whistle in my sleep. God forgive me;
> forgive all of us who called ourselves Christians yet did noth-
> ing to intervene.[13]

Similarly, many Christians in America often think, naively, that there is nothing they can do to stop the cultural landslide that is happening before their eyes, so they sit inside the church and sing louder and louder, seeming to hope the train will go away. We are called to get outside the four walls of the church and preach the gospel with boldness to all generations—with power from on high—not fearing the consequences, but simply maintaining a calm assurance that Jesus will always be with us (Matthew 28:20). Yes, we stand before a tough opponent. But let us remember that he who is in us is greater than he who is in the world (1 John 4:4).

I'll Be Back

In every movie in which Arnold Schwarzenegger has starred—*Conan the Barbarian, The Terminator, Total Recall*—he meets his opponent, he fights, and he wins. As I sat in that meeting in the spring of 2009, I thought about Arnold, the media, and Hollywood—and it occurred to me that they're winning. They're winning this battle. The culture is influencing the church rather than the church impacting the culture.

The other pastors and I sat and talked with the governor that day about some of our nation's current core issues. We asked him point-blank about his stance regarding same-sex marriage. He gave us the politically correct response by saying that he personally believed that marriage is between a man and woman. "But," he said, "I also think that anybody has the right to marry anybody that he or she wants."

And that's when the pastor to his right, Miles McPherson, asked

unleashed

28

him, "Well, what if two men want to marry two women?" We wanted the governor to carry out his line of logic that, if anybody has the right to marry anybody, what keeps two men from marrying two women and the four of them calling it a marriage? Governor Schwarzenegger thought about it for a moment and then agreed that two men ought to be able to marry two women.

> Our culture is confused about what is right and wrong, and the church is confused about whether it is our "job" to speak out.

Here's the point: this is precisely where we're headed if the churches and individual Christians who have lost their purpose and power don't return to their roles as part of the worldwide church—the same church of the New Testament. Our culture is confused about what is right and wrong, and the church is confused about whether it is our "job" to speak out. But we have seen clear instruction from the Word of God that, since the Holy Spirit has been released upon the church, the church must be unleashed upon the world to influence, preach boldly, and speak the truth in love.

Equipped with the power of the Holy Spirit, we are to go and be salt in all arenas of life—seasoning the culture, transforming lives, and glorifying God until Christ comes again. Over the course of this book and through further examination of the church we find in Acts, we will uncover the specific steps we can take to truly emulate the powerful and effective first-century church in order to impact and engage the world in Christ's name. We will see that, like a precious, multifaceted jewel, the same brilliant qualities the church reflected in the New Testament are the same pillars we must recapture today:

- By fulfilling the Great Commission in reaching out to all nations and people groups, despite racial or ethnic differences, we will become a

unleashed

kaleidoscope that attracts the whole world to the church's welcoming beauty and diversity (Acts 1:8; 10:1-48).

- When we minister faithfully to the multitudes, we will see *innumerable* souls won for the kingdom of God (Acts 2:41-47; 4:4).

- We will see *pandemonium* ensue as others, including religious and political authorities, take notice of the excitement and commotion of God's church working in their midst (Acts 4:13-22).

- When the church is bathed in prayer, we will be *shaken* by the power of God's Spirit and preach fearlessly and without restraint (Acts 4:23-31).

- We will demonstrate *lavishness* when we see the needs of those around us, give sacrificially, and are willing to give up anything and everything to see the church impact the world (Acts 4:32-37).

- If we continue to proclaim the good news, despite risk or danger, we will display a *hazardous* faith and rejoice in being counted worthy of suffering for the name of Jesus Christ (Acts 5:17-42).

- Our eyes will be opened to the *kinetic* power of the gospel—a supernatural energy that converts potential into reality, even in the face of rejection or opposition (Acts 13:41-52).

- Finally, we will take hold of the *unequivocal* calling to go into the whole world, regardless of hardship, and testify about the good news of salvation to a lost and dying world (Acts 20:22-24).

It's my prayer and hope that God will energize the church and transform it into what he truly envisions it to be—not an entity that walks in confusion and weakness, but a powerful force, galvanized by the Holy Spirit much like our brothers and sisters in the first century were. May we together stand when others are falling, may we finish the race, may we complete the task, and may we remain focused on calling the church to turn the world upside down!

kaleidoscope

Acts 1:8; 10:1-48

Many young people who have grown up in the Xbox generation might not have a clue about what a kaleidoscope is. A kaleidoscope is a simple cylinder that contains mirrors and many multicolored beads and pieces of glass and plastic. It has a viewing hole on one end. As you look through it, you will see a wonderful display of colors and limitless patterns that change every time you reposition it.

The kaleidoscope derives its name from three ancient Greek words, which are translated into English as "beautiful," "form," and "observing tool."[1] So a kaleidoscope literally means "observer of beautiful forms." Perhaps God has a kaleidoscope in Heaven that he enjoys looking through, and as he does he sees us humans—the beautiful forms.

After God made the universe and mankind, the Bible says, "God saw all that he made, and it was very good" (Genesis 1:31). God was thrilled with his entire creation, but he was extra delighted in his special creation, mankind—because man was made in God's very image (v. 27).

When God created the first man and woman, he gave them the DNA that would give birth to a world populated with people of all shapes, sizes, and colors. Luke says, "From one man he made all the nations, that they should inhabit the whole earth; and he marked out their appointed times in history and the boundaries of their lands" (Acts 17:26). We may live in different places, speak different languages, and have different shades of skin, but the fact is that we all are descendants of that first couple, and therefore, we all belong to one race—the human race.

The church in Acts encompassed people of all nations. But the process of becoming a church that reached all people wasn't instantaneous.

God's Spirit had to move in the hearts of the apostles to prod them to overcome the barriers that divided people in their day. Similarly, I pray that this chapter will also encourage you to boldly follow God's lead in your heart, as he calls you to go beyond racial and cultural zones in your life and ministry.

A Good Day to Start the Church

In the spring of AD 30, a multinational gathering of Jews (and converts to Judaism) filled the streets of Jerusalem to celebrate the Jewish holiday Pentecost (Acts 2:1, 5, 9-11). This was the day the apostles had been waiting for—the day the Holy Spirit would come upon them with power. Jesus couldn't have chosen a better day to unleash his church.

Before the day was over, three thousand people had accepted the message and were baptized (v. 41). On day one Jesus' church was a multinational, multilingual megachurch of Jewish believers. Can you imagine being in a church like that? It was colorful, vibrant, and exciting—a true kaleidoscope.

Jewish believers had never associated themselves with Samaritans in the past.

Luke's inspired account goes on to tell the remarkable story of how the church advanced geographically and culturally. In Acts 6 the church wisely resolved a conflict between the Grecian Jewish believers and Hebraic Jewish believers. In Acts 8 the church advanced into Samaria. This was big because the Jewish believers had never associated themselves with Samaritans in the past. Additionally in Acts 8, Luke related the story of how an Ethiopian government official came to faith in Jesus and was baptized.

As the Word of God spread through Jerusalem, Judea, and Samaria, it was clear that Jesus' final directives to the apostles were being fulfilled. God was doing something amazing. Jesus had promised his followers,

"You will receive power when the Holy Spirit comes on you; and you will be my witnesses in Jerusalem, and in all Judea and Samaria, and to the ends of the earth" (Acts 1:8) . . . and it was coming true.

Breaking the Gentile Barrier

Approximately seven years after the church's beginning, the one barrier that had not been broken was the Gentile barrier. The followers of Jesus had not yet actively taken the gospel to non-Jews, so the Spirit had to intervene and do what the Spirit loves to do—open the doors to people's hearts and inspire the disciples to spread the Word.

During New Testament times the big race problem wasn't about skin tone, as it is today; it was about the dividing wall of hostility that separated people of Jewish heritage from the Gentiles. The rich history

> One negative consequence of being "chosen" is the temptation to become arrogant.

of the Jews made them a proud and distinctive people. The Jewish nation was in fact God's chosen people—the circumcised, the keepers of the law, and the sons of Abraham. Jesus himself was Jewish.

But one negative consequence of being "chosen" is the temptation to become arrogant. Now, there *were* Old Testament laws intended to keep Jews separated from the outside influence of false religion. But by the time of Jesus, zealous Jews, in their self-righteous pride, had become prejudiced and hostile—something God never intended. They felt superior to Gentiles (Romans 2:17; 3:1, 2). So for nearly a decade, the church only included people who had Jewish backgrounds—with the exception of the converts to Judaism who were present on the Day of Pentecost. But God wasn't done yet.

Hold your place here for a few minutes and pause to read Acts 10. It tells the inspiring account of how God opened the door of the kingdom to the Gentiles.

unleashed

Peter and Cornelius

God selected Peter to convert the first Gentiles. After all, Jesus had given him the "keys of the kingdom" (Matthew 16:19). But before that could happen, God had to deal with Peter's prejudices. That's right, the great apostle Peter—who boldly proclaimed the risen Savior in Jerusalem, Judea, and Samaria—was hesitant to embrace the Gentiles. To get Peter's attention the Lord spoke to him in a vision:

> About noon the following day as they were on their journey and approaching the city, Peter went up on the roof to pray. He became hungry and wanted something to eat, and while the meal was being prepared, he fell into a trance. He saw heaven opened and something like a large sheet being let down to earth by its four corners. It contained all kinds of four-footed animals, as well as reptiles and birds. Then a voice told him, "Get up, Peter. Kill and eat."
>
> "Surely not, Lord!" Peter replied. "I have never eaten anything impure or unclean."
>
> The voice spoke to him a second time, "Do not call anything impure that God has made clean."
>
> This happened three times, and immediately the sheet was taken back to heaven" (Acts 10:9-16).

The number three wasn't Peter's favorite number. I'm sure it reminded him of his least favorite animal, the rooster, but it did get Peter thinking. While Peter was trying to figure out and interpret the meaning of the vision, strangers approached the gate and asked for Peter.

The day before Peter received his vision, the Lord had sent an angel to Cornelius, who told him to send some men to Joppa and bring back Peter to Caesarea. Cornelius was an Italian officer in Roman military; he and all his family were God-fearing and fervent. The Bible says that he gave charitably to those in need and he prayed to God habitually. There was one caveat, however; he was an unclean, impure, and uncircumcised Gentile. Nevertheless, the Lord had chosen him to be the first Gentile in God's kaleidoscopic kingdom.

When Peter went outside to meet Cornelius's men, they explained to him how an angel had spoken to Cornelius and told him to send for Peter. Peter welcomed them all in; and the following morning they, along with some other brothers, started their journey to Caesarea to meet with Cornelius. When they stopped for the night, I'm sure Peter didn't sleep well, as he was still trying to figure out what God was up to.

Overcoming Prejudice

Sometime the following day they arrived at Cornelius's place in Caesarea. Peter was about to do something he had never done—enter the home of a Gentile. I can only imagine what was going on in Peter's mind as he entered the home and smelled the aroma of the Italian food, realizing he was breaking all kinds of Jewish laws. As he looked around, he saw a house filled wall-to-wall with Gentiles, all close friends and relatives of Cornelius. Peter's introductory remarks revealed what was heavy on his heart. He said, "You are well aware that it is against our law for a Jew to associate with or visit a Gentile. But God has shown me that I should not call anyone impure or unclean. So when I was sent for, I came without raising any objection. May I ask why you sent for me?" (Acts 10:28, 29).

That's an unusual and rather awkward way to start a sermon. Even so, Peter openly confessed his prejudicial feelings. He went on to say, "I now realize how true it is that God does not show favoritism but accepts from every nation the one who fears him and does what is right" (vv. 34, 35).

unleashed

Peter finally understood the full meaning of the vision. It wasn't about eating lizards or snakes or . . . chitlins. It was about Peter's bigotry. The way Peter felt about eating unclean food was really how he felt about the Gentiles. The Lord was telling Peter to love Gentiles, to treat them as equals, and even more than that—to reach them with the gospel.

> The Lord was telling Peter to love Gentiles, to treat them as equals, and even more than that—to reach them with the gospel.

While Peter was preaching, and as the Gentile audience was coming to faith in Jesus, God settled the matter of the acceptance of the Gentiles once and for all—not just for Peter's sake but also for the brothers who had come with Peter. They would later have to explain their actions to the other brothers. The Holy Spirit disrupted Peter's sermon with an event similar to what happened to the disciples on the Day of Pentecost. The Gentiles were miraculously speaking in tongues. Can't you picture Peter with a wry smile on his face, asking the brothers with him, "Any objections?"

Peter ordered that these Gentiles be immersed in water. The Gentiles were now accepted into the kaleidoscopic kingdom.

Restore the Mission—to *All Nations*

When God was selecting David to succeed Saul as king of Israel, he said to Samuel, "The LORD does not look at the things people look at. People look at the outward appearance, but the LORD looks at the heart" (1 Samuel 16:7). The apostles were slow to understand the scope of Jesus' mission because their prejudices had blinded them to seeing people from God's point of view.

Our society is preoccupied with external looks, isn't it? People today obsess over superficial matters like the color of skin. Fair-skinned people can make themselves bronze through tan from a bottle, whereas some darker-skinned people have been known to bleach their skin white. Go figure.

God doesn't care about the color of our skin; he cares about the condition of our hearts. He's interested in our inner being, our souls, and our salvation. That's why Jesus commanded the apostles (and disciples today) to spread the good news of the grace of God to everyone in every nation. The subject of the mission was clear—all people. Not just the Jewish nation, but *all nations.* The New Testament mentions this Great Commission several times:

> God doesn't care about the color of our skin; he cares about the condition of our hearts.

- "Go and make disciples of *all nations*" (Matthew 28:19).
- "Go into all the world and preach the gospel to *all creation*" (Mark 16:15).
- "Repentance for the forgiveness of sins will be preached in his name to *all nations,* beginning at Jerusalem" (Luke 24:47).
- "You will receive power when the Holy Spirit comes on you; and you will be my witnesses in Jerusalem, and in all Judea and Samaria, and to *the ends of the earth*" (Acts 1:8, emphasis added in all).

If the apostles could be so easily distracted from what was so important to Jesus, it isn't shocking that modern-day followers of Jesus can misunderstand the content and importance of Jesus' mission as well. I believe every generation of followers of Jesus should renew their convictions, readjust their focus, and restore their commitment to Jesus' mission. Because Jesus is the same today as he was yesterday, his desire remains the same. He still wants *all* people in *all* nations to come to know God. That's why it's imperative that his followers be united in heart (John 17:21).

unleashed

Unity is a great witness for God, just as much as disunity is a great witness for Satan. Instigating racial disunity is one of Satan's favorite strategies for sowing seeds of doubt. He knows it hurts the testimony of the church.

> Instigating racial disunity is one of Satan's favorite strategies for sowing seeds of doubt. He knows it hurts the testimony of the church.

In 1963, Dr. Martin Luther King Jr. stated during a speech at Western Michigan University, "We must face the fact that in America, the church is still the most segregated major institution in America. At 11:00 on Sunday morning when we stand and sing and Christ has no east or west, we stand at the most segregated hour in this nation. This is tragic. Nobody of honesty can overlook this."[2]

I wonder how today's Christians would respond to Dr. King's concerns. Does his statement still ring true? Has the enemy of our souls deceived us into thinking that Jesus' ongoing desire for unity (including racial harmony) in the body of Christ is an unrealistic dream—and not worth our time, prayers, and efforts?

Restore the New Command—the Jesus Standard of Love

"A new command I give you: Love one another. *As I have loved you,* so you must love one another. By this everyone will know that you are my disciples, if you love one another" (John 13:34, 35, emphasis added). Take a moment and ask yourself:

- Do I fellowship with Christians from different ethnic backgrounds?
- Am I hesitant to evangelize people of other cultural groups?
- Are all my deep spiritual relationships with people of my own race?
- Am I bitter toward people of other races?

Jesus taught that our love for one another would serve as a strong witness to the unbelieving world that we are genuine followers of Jesus. The opposite is also true. When we mistreat, look down on, and dislike others (especially based only on the color of skin), the world will question the authenticity of our discipleship.

For centuries Christians have sought to restore Jesus' church by emphasizing teachings concerning church doctrine, church polity, and worship practices, among other things. However, in my opinion, what hasn't been emphasized adequately is the restoration of the Jesus standard of love for one another—the kind of love that can break through barriers that divide people by groups, including the walls of racial division.

I love the old motto quoted by many in our fellowship of churches, "In essentials, unity; in nonessentials, liberty; in all things, love." Unfortunately, when this slogan was commonly recited many years ago, people from West Africa were inhumanely being shipped like cargo to be sold as slaves in America . . . to some of the same people who loved to quote that motto.

In reference to the 1851 annual report of the American and Foreign Anti-Slavery Society, Garrison and DeGroot write, in *The Disciples of Christ: A History,* that the Disciples (often called Campbellites at that time) owned 101,000 slaves. If the math is right, that means that the Disciples, on a per capita basis, constituted the leading slave-holding church in the nation.[3]

When I first came to realize that my distant spiritual forefathers participated in slavery, I was disheartened. But I was encouraged to discover how God's Spirit actively worked to move in the hearts of Christian leaders in that era. For instance, consider Barton Stone, the key leader in the Christian revival movement in Kentucky. Because of his fervent commitment to the restoration of New Testament Christianity, he and his followers came to the conviction that they must free and support the slaves

unleashed

they had previously owned. He and his followers began to strongly preach against the institution of slavery, as he preached about the kingdom.

Lawrence Burnley writes in his book *The Cost of Unity*, "Stone eventually became outspoken in his opposition to slavery. Concerning his changed opinion, leading to the release of those he held in captivity, Stone credited his experience during the revivals at Cane Ridge as a turning point in his life."[4] Today's Christians should never forget:

- that God's Word has the power to change our hearts (Hebrews 4:12).
- that our battle is not against flesh and blood—it's against our adversary, Satan (Ephesians 6:12).
- that Jesus, the Great Physician, is the only one who can heal the wounds in our soul and our nation (Isaiah 53:5).

As I read my Bible today, and as I listen to God's Spirit in my heart, I am compelled to recommit to obey Jesus' new command to love others just like Jesus loves me. My motivation is simple: I just want to hear Jesus say to me, "Daryl, well done." What I never want to hear Jesus say to me is, "Daryl, you have neglected the more important matters of the law—justice, mercy and faithfulness. You should have practiced the latter, without neglecting the former" (see Matthew 23:23).

It's simply not OK to have our doctrines right while our hearts toward others are wrong.

I believe God's Spirit wants to do something big in our day, perhaps initiating another revival movement that focuses on unleashing love to a wounded world and resulting in turning the world upside down. For the past two decades, I've witnessed God incrementally unleashing his kaleidoscope kingdom in the hearts of many Christians.

If you are a follower of Jesus, will you join me in recommitting to obeying Jesus' most vital and new command to really love one another?

A Peek Through My Kaleidoscope

God has a way of grabbing our attention. Allow me to share with you how God expanded my vision and helped prepare me to minister to all nations. Through the years many people have inspired me to become a barrier-breaking Christian, and I want to share some of their stories with you as well.

If You Have Jesus in Common, You Have Everything in Common

I was eighteen years old when I visited a small church in rural, west central Illinois. Macomb is a college town, home to Western Illinois University, where I attended as a student athlete. I was raised in a predominantly African-American congregation in the city of Milwaukee, Wisconsin, and I had a feeling that attending church in a rural community was going to give me a unique experience.

It did.

The church building was located on the outskirts of town, over a mile and a half from the dorm where I stayed. My walk to church took me past a small cornfield; that was very different for me. As I entered the modest church building, I realized I was the only black person there. The color of skin wasn't the only thing that struck me as dissimilar. I noticed some of the men wore blue-jeans overalls, work boots, and flannel shirts. They all spoke with the same small-town mid-American accent. The congregational singing was different too. They sang a cappella, which I was familiar with, but their singing was more "by the book." The soulful, harmonic ad-libbing I was used to was absent.

> As I entered the modest church building, I realized I was the only black person there.

unleashed

Although the people were different, I got connected anyway. Why? Because of love.

I felt more than welcome. The members were very hospitable. They opened up their hearts as well as their homes. I think they knew the quickest way to the heart of a college student was through his stomach. During a critical time in my life, being away from home for the first time, that small congregation of believers had a profound impact on me.

I still have fond memories of the families there. I am especially grateful for the minister of the congregation, John Sullivan. His love, humility, and devotion to God's Word caused me to say to a friend about him, "I think he is the most Jesus-like person I ever met."

Together we started a Bible discussion group in my dorm room. It grew rapidly, spawning several other small groups on campus. Many of my teammates, roommates, and friends attended regularly, and some of them became members of the church and were baptized—including my future wife, Charon.

I learned a lot about evangelism, discipling relationships, and building ministries during those years. However, the greatest lesson I learned was that God is able to use *anyone* to reach *anyone*. When you have Jesus in common, you have everything in common.

Today John is still doing in Iowa what he did in Illinois back in the early '80s—serving, loving, and ministering to a diverse congregation. I owe a debt of love to that church in Macomb; it gave me my start in the ministry. Since then I've been privileged to serve in Great Commission–minded congregations in the Midwest, Southern California, and now on the East Coast in the Washington, DC, area.

Today I am blessed to serve as a preaching minister in DC Regional Christian Church, a congregation that meets in Forestville, Maryland. Our congregation reflects the diversity of our area. We have blacks, whites, Asians, and Hispanics; and many of our members were born in other countries around the world, especially in Africa and the Caribbean Islands. Our senior leadership group and our community group leaders reflect the same diversity.

God has blessed me abundantly with diverse friendships; some are old friends like John Sullivan. Some are relatively new, like my friendship and partnership in the gospel with Ben Cachiaras, a pastor of a growing congregation in Hartford County, Maryland. Mountain Christian Church dates back to the early 1800s. Ben's prayer and commitment to move beyond racial zones led to the two of us getting connected. John, Ben, and I—though we are very different—have everything in common through Jesus.

> The greatest lesson I learned was that God is able to use *anyone* to reach *anyone*.

The Greatest Gift I Received Was a Powerful Example

I feel spiritually blessed because I grew up in a Christian family. Being equipped for ministry started early for me. The dream of being a preacher was planted in my heart through the example of my grandfather, Quiller Harris (I call him Hey-Hey). As my minister, he baptized me, mentored me, and officiated at my wedding. His devotion to God and his heart for serving others has always inspired me to want to be a minister of the gospel. He was, and is, a hard-working servant, a frugal steward, and a wise counselor. His example and devotion to God's Word have been chiseled into my convictions.

My grandfather is a barrier-breaking Christian. Born and raised in Louisiana, he grew up very poor in an age when blacks were considered by many to be second-class citizens. As a result, my grandfather experienced injustices that were commonplace. When he was a child, his family took in an older woman who at one time had been a slave. My

unleashed

grandfather could've easily become embittered against whites. But mainly due to his faith in God, he didn't.

I'm still inspired by the friendship he has with a fellow retired preacher in Milwaukee. Brother Monroe Hawley ministered to a predominantly white congregation on the west side, and my grandfather ministered to communities on the northeast side of Milwaukee. Through their relationship, and along with the influence of my grandmother, God used their lives and friendship to help initiate new congregations in Milwaukee. Their mutual respect for one another serves as a model for how to break through racial barriers.

> If he had a close friendship with a white Christian brother to help advance God's kingdom, I knew that I could too.

As an African-American male, I have experienced discrimination. However, my negative experiences are small compared to those from my grandfather's generation. If he had a close friendship with a white Christian brother to help advance God's kingdom, I knew that I could too.

I am convinced that the greatest gift we can pass on to the next generation is the priceless gift of a Christlike example. So Hey-Hey, thanks for your tremendous example!

Love People and Point Them to Jesus

Kevin Holland is another man God used to inspire me to be a barrier-breaking Christian. In 1989, Kevin invited me to join a church plant in metropolitan Detroit. My girlfriend was finishing school, and I was eager for the mission adventure. A group numbering about twenty-five signed up for the church-planting team. It was comprised of whites, blacks, and an Asian guy—who became my roommate. From the onset we had a desire to build a multiracial, Great Commission–minded congregation.

Kevin's ability to connect with all kinds of people really stood out to me. He had a wonderful way of making people feel loved and accepted, without passing judgment on them. Although Kevin has a very engaging personality, and though he is very intelligent and gifted in many ways, he never made the ministry about himself; he constantly pointed people to Jesus.

It was amazing to be a part of a diverse group of friends who were passionate about reaching all nations for Christ. That first year over one hundred people from all walks of life were baptized into Christ. At the end of the first year, Kevin asked me to join him in the full-time preaching ministry. I was only too eager to resign from my job selling computers, and I've been in the full-time preaching ministry ever since. Today Kevin still serves as a spiritual mentor to me. And God is still using him in powerful ways as the lead evangelist of Turning Point Christian Church, a multiracial congregation in Southern California.

Nothing (Including Racial Reconciliation) Is Impossible with God

Another close friend of mine is a man of Polish descent. Ron Drabot is the minister who officially ordained and appointed me to be an evangelist for ministry.

In the early 1990s, Ron led a small mission team to Johannesburg, South Africa. They had a seemingly impossible dream of building a multiracial congregation in the land of apartheid, the government policy that legalized and enforced racial segregation. Through the new ministry, white South Africans and black South Africans were baptized, showing that the mission wasn't impossible after all. "Coincidentally" in 1994, the demeaning and discriminating government policy that enforced racial segregation had finally come to an end, and Nelson Mandela was elected the first president of the post-apartheid era.

unleashed

I had the privilege of seeing the congregation firsthand in the '90s. It was truly one of the most faith-building and encouraging experiences I've ever had. It was nothing less than a miracle to see with my own eyes white South Africans and black South Africans worshipping together in true Christian unity. Today the Johannesburg International Church of Christ is a kaleidoscopic congregation of over twelve hundred members. Through the power of God, dozens of other similar congregations have been planted throughout the continent.

If we asked Ron today, "What's the greatest need of our hour?" no doubt he would answer, "Prayer—tapping into God's power." Why? Because when we rely on our own power, we burn out, become ineffective, and eventually quit. But great things can be accomplished when we rely on God's limitless supply of power.

> God's powerful kaleidoscopic kingdom *is* being unleashed.

Breaking through racial zones in ministry might seem naive and unrealistic, or even impossible. But the Bible says, "With God all things are possible" (Matthew 19:26). "Nothing is impossible with God" (Luke 1:37, *NLT*).

I want to encourage you to never quit and to never stop praying (Luke 18:1) toward the end of achieving racial reconciliation in the church.

Before Jesus commanded his disciples to "go," he first commanded them to "wait," to wait for God's power (Acts 1:4). His power has come, and we can walk in it. God's powerful kaleidoscopic kingdom *is* being unleashed. The only question is, will you partner with Jesus in building that visible kingdom on earth?

"After this I looked, and there before me was a great multitude that no one could count, from every nation, tribe, people and language, standing before the throne and before the Lamb" (Revelation 7:9).

innumerable

Acts 2:41-47; 4:4

After you read each of the following statements, say the word *innumerable* out loud (unless there are people around you. Then just say it in your head).

- grains of sand on the seashore
- stars in the sky
- drops of water in the sea
- tears a mother will cry
- number of times a four-year-old will ask "Why . . . ?"
- number of games the Cleveland Browns have lost (I'm a die-hard Browns fan, so I can make this joke.)

Many things seem beyond counting.

Here's something else that appears to be beyond counting.

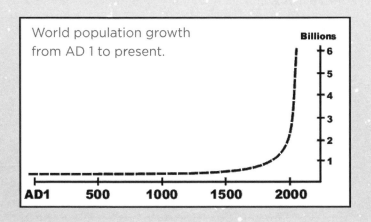

World population growth from AD 1 to present.

Notice that from AD 1 until about AD 1600, the world population stayed flat at around one billion people.[1] Now let's add two lines that represent the life span of our generation.

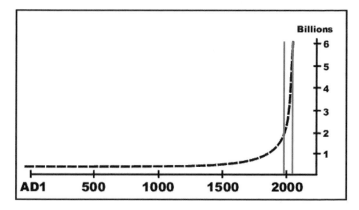

Notice that in our lifetime alone world population has grown from approximately two billion people to more than six billion![2] In our lifetime! (You can shout "Innumerable!")

Good News and Bad News

Next, let's compare the growth of Christianity with the growth of the world's population.

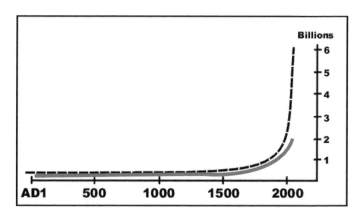

From zero to more than two billion Christians in two thousand years![3] Very encouraging. In fact, in the early days of Christianity, the growth of the number of Jesus' followers could be described as innumerable!

- Acts 1:15 begins with 120 followers of Jesus.
- In Acts 2:41 the number multiplied to more than 3,000.
- Acts 2:47 tells us that more and more people were responding to the good news of Jesus Christ *every day*.
- A short period of time later, Acts 4:4 records that "about" 5,000 men were now Christians.
- Acts 5:14 continues by asserting that "more and more men and women believed in the Lord and were added to their number."
- Acts 6:1 says, "The number of disciples was increasing."
- Acts 9:31 records this amazing statement: "Living in the fear of the Lord and encouraged by the Holy Spirit, [the church] increased in numbers."

By AD 350 there were thirty-one million Christians, more than half the population of the Roman Empire![4] The church was growing so rapidly that it became virtually impossible to count. Innumerable!

> By AD 350 there were thirty-one million Christians, more than half the population of the Roman Empire!

That's good news!

Next, let's take a look at the data for the United States of America. Only 23 percent of Americans are "regular participants" in the life of the church. (A regular participant is defined as "a person who attends church at least three out of every eight Sundays"—not a very rigorous standard.) Think about that. "Seventy-seven percent of Americans do not have a consistent, life-giving connection with a local church."[5]

unleashed

Furthermore, virtually every recent study conducted on Christianity in the United States reveals that the number of adherents to the good news of Jesus Christ is in serious decline!

Umm . . . not so encouraging.

And here's why this is a problem: God "wants all people to be saved and to come to a knowledge of the truth" (1 Timothy 2:4). So why hasn't the expansion of Christianity kept pace with the expansion of the world's population? The number of followers of Jesus grew exponentially for the first three hundred years after Jesus' death and resurrection. So rather than continuing on the same trend, why has that growth rate faltered?

Put on your thinking cap with me. Sound like school? We're going to get into a bit of *ology* study. In fact, the suffix *ology* is derived from the Greek word *logia* and means "field of study."[6] So if you're studying biology, you're studying what? Living things. If you're studying sociology, you're studying the interaction of humans in society. Geology? The physical earth. How about latrinology? Latrinology is the study of writing on bathroom walls (I'm not making this up). Piscatology? The study of fishing (any Pisces reading this?). And philematology? The study of kissing[7] (so if your teenager says she's going to her boyfriend's house to study philematology—beware).

What does all this *ology* stuff have to do with the expansion of Christianity in an innumerable way? Everything!

Christology > Missiology > Ecclesiology

In the early church, Christology (what we believe about Jesus) determined missiology (what we believe about the church's mission), which in turn determined ecclesiology (how the church must function). And since Jesus was all about proclaiming his good news so that people could be saved (Luke 19:10), the mission of the followers of Jesus must be to proclaim the good news so that people can be saved (Matthew 28:19). Therefore, the primary function of the church should be to seek and save the lost.[8]

Unfortunately, around AD 325, the order of things started getting out of whack. In 313, Emperor Constantine had legalized Christian worship and embedded Christianity in the political arena. Christians, for the first time, enjoyed not only the freedom to worship in public but also high standing and influence in society.

So what did the church do with its newfound good fortune? It built cathedrals. Massive, beautiful edifices where people could come to experience God, receive religious services, and learn about Jesus. Sounds good, right? Wrong! The church was no longer following the correct order of Christology determining missiology determining ecclesiology. It had reoriented to ecclesiology determining missiology determining Christology. And that had huge ramifications on how effectively the good news continued to spread and how people became disciples of Jesus.

> The church was no longer following the correct order of Christology determining missiology determining ecclesiology.

Wrong Order: Ecclesiology > Missiology > Christology

Since AD 325, one of the primary initiatives of the church has been to put up buildings so that people will "come." By believing that buildings are central to the church, it's possible that the mission of the church can become all about putting up larger and better buildings—which in turn will direct (even if by default) what is taught about Jesus. Alan Hirsch said, "Christianity was at its most effective and most true to its nature as the people of God when it did not own any buildings."[9]

unleashed

To be fair, I must say that I know of some examples in which a bigger church building was necessary because of the number of lost people who were being reached in a community. I believe that buildings in and of themselves are not evil. If a church is reaching many souls for Christ by doing all the right things, and if erecting a larger building is absolutely necessary for the continued grow of the kingdom of God in that area, then I'm for it.

From a historical perspective, the comments that follow pertain to the extravagant abuse that has taken place in the past, and unfortunately, continues to affect many of our churches in the present. Those new church building campaigns led to at least three contributing factors that slowed the spread of the good news of Jesus Christ:

1. Building cathedrals costs a lot of money. The mission of the church became keeping the financial engine of the church running. And what was taught about Jesus was driven by the church's need to pay its bills.
2. When cathedrals were built and the church gained power in the community, the church began to flex its muscle in the political arena. Not only was morality legislated, but Christians began to believe that Christianity should be legislated as well. Historically, this meant that positions of leadership within the church (because of the political power they wielded) began to be bought and sold to the highest bidder. The hope of the world should have been Jesus, through his followers; but that was replaced with the power of the church exercised through the government.
3. When cathedrals became the largest buildings in the community, at the center of the community, they became a provider of services for the community. People came to market at the cathedral (markets were typically set up around the church building), where they could also have their children baptized, demons exorcised, and sins exonerated! A one-stop shop. The Christian consumer mentality began to take shape.

Thank goodness we've left all that behind . . . or have we? I contend that the same misalignment of ecclesiology determining missiology determining Christology (which decimated the effectiveness and the innumerable growth of the followers of Jesus) is alive and well in our Western culture and, specifically, within the communities of the United States.

> This new building, which houses thousands of Christians, can wield enormous political influence.

Outside of new church plants, the fastest-growing churches in North America today are the megachurches (churches of two thousand people or more in weekend attendance).[10] And a megachurch most often puts up a massive building or "campus" in order to reach thousands of people. (I know because I have led a megachurch for the past twenty years.) This new building, which houses thousands of Christians, can wield enormous political influence as it continues to provide wonderful religious services. In other words, ecclesiology determining missiology determining Christology.

I don't intend to go on a mega-bashing rampage of the megachurch— I have also been involved in smaller churches whose mission and Christology were determined in the same fashion. Virtually all of Western Christianity has been infected by Constantine's virus. The results of this kind of ecclesiology determining missiology determining Christology are almost identical in outcome to the malaise of the church in the Dark Ages.

1. Church buildings must be paid for. The financial engine must be kept running. This has huge implications for what we teach about the mission of the church and, therefore, what we teach about Jesus. Ever hear (or say) phrases like these?

unleashed

- "Bring your friends *to* church."
- "Your primary financial generosity is *to* the church."
- "Your first place to serve is *within* the church."

2. When the church wields power in the community political arena, it follows that people begin to place their hope in the local government rather than in Jesus as lived out through his church. (I do believe that followers of Jesus should be involved in legislating morality, but not in legislating Christianity.) This is played out in phrases like this:

- "We are God's chosen nation. God bless the USA."
- "God helps us win wars because God is on our side."
- "We are a Christian nation, perhaps more so than others."

3. When the church becomes a place rather than a people, it becomes a provider of religious services—and this feeds into a devastating consumer mind-set found among most Christians. This is played out in phrases like this (either thought or spoken):

- "I go to church to be spiritually fed."
- "I take my children to church so that someone else can be given the responsibility for developing their faith in Jesus."
- "The style of music needs to please me, or I'll simply find another church that better fits my personal preference."

I'd like to point out that those bad attitudes don't exist *only* within large churches. They can also be seen in small groups of ten people meeting in someone's living room. But perhaps it's easier to think these kinds of things when so many services are provided for us in the larger church.

The Remedy for Ecclesiology > Missiology > Christology

The end result of this inverted process, simply put, is that the number of followers of Jesus is no longer growing at an innumerable rate.

But there's good news! The antidote to the virus that began in the era of Constantine is simply to return to Christology determining our missiology determining our ecclesiology. In other words, if we

> The number of followers of Jesus is no longer growing at an innumerable rate.

can regain a right understanding of the life purpose of Jesus, then our mission will be determined as well, which will radically revolutionize the form and function—and effectiveness—of the church!

So let's take a look at the life purpose of Jesus, where it all begins. Christology. "For God so loved the world that he gave his one and only Son, that whoever believes in him shall not perish but have eternal life. For God did not send his Son into the world to condemn the world, but to save the world through him" (John 3:16, 17). Not to condemn or judge the world but to save the world. God is *for* people. That's good news!

God is *for* people, but most people don't realize this and, in fact, actually believe that God is against them.

Why do so many people believe that God is against them? Well, in part, we Christians are to blame. I've seen sign after sign in front of

unleashed

churches that say things like, "If you have had an abortion, then you are a murderer" or "God hates divorce." What message does that send to people?

Most of us don't carry around signs that scream, "God hates fags!" But our attitudes, our jokes, and our lack of inclusion, scream the same message.

And of course, some Christians put bumper stickers like these on their cars: "One nation under God. Accept it or leave!" Or "After the rapture you can have this car." And my personal favorite, "Every time you vote Democrat, God kills a kitten."

If God really is *for* people, would he want his followers sending those kinds of messages on his behalf?

This past fall, just as school was beginning, a Christian school in our area launched a billboard campaign to market their educational community. The billboard image was a picture of a classroom with children smiling warmly. The caption on the billboard simply stated, "Come to our school where God will be with your children." Which implies what? That God is *not* with the kids whose parents have them in public school?

Ask yourself: *What message am I sending to people who are far away from God? From watching my life, do people know that God is* for *them?*

Now let's return to Christology, because there's even better news: God isn't only for us; he is *with* us. We see this beginning in the Old Testament. God was with the nation of Israel as a cloud by day and a pillar of fire by night. God was with Moses as he spoke to him from a burning bush. God was with Daniel in the lions' den. We could go on and on, but ultimately the idea of God with us becomes reality in Immanuel. God, in Jesus, is with us (Matthew 1:23).

When people realize that God is *with* them, some still reply with sadness. Because of their view of God being "against" them—God with a big stick—they tend to respond with fear to God being with them. God being *with* us is certainly better than God being *for* us, but we must be careful not to send messages like these to people who are far from God:

- "I'm for you, but I'm not going to be with you until you clean up your act."
- "I'm happy to be with you . . . if you want to come to my church this weekend."
- "You are welcome to be with me after you change your lifestyle."

And in the end, nobody wants to be with us! Or more tragically, no one wants to be with the God we represent!

But it doesn't stop there. There's even better news: in Jesus, God becomes *one of* us. The apostle Paul said, "For in Christ lives all the fullness of God in a human body" (Colossians 2:9, *NLT*). Jesus lives as *one of* us, loves as *one of* us, even "likes" us while he is *one of* us.

 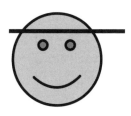

As good as it is to know that God is for us and with us, it amazes us that God is *one of* us . . . and that he actually *likes* us!

This is important. We aren't *for, with,* and *one of* people because they are our targets. No one wants to be someone's little project. With Jesus in us we can be for, with, and one of people because we actually *like* them. Why do we like them? Because Jesus likes them!

There are four words in the Greek language that we translate into English as the word *love:*

- *storge* = family love
- *eros* = sensual love
- *philos* = friendship love
- *agape* = unconditional love[11]

When Jesus was crucified, it wasn't because of whom he loved. In Matthew 11:19 Jesus was accused of *liking* sinners. The Greek word is *philos.* The Pharisees of Jesus' day might have endured a mission by Jesus that was all about *agape*—unconditional love for tax collectors and sinners; and Christ's mission certainly included unconditional love. But for Jesus, *agape* went hand in hand with *philos.* And "liking" sinners couldn't be tolerated. The Pharisees didn't accuse Jesus of loving sinners; they accused him of liking them, of being their friend.

> Are people who are far away from God drawn to you because Jesus is in you, and they actually like you?

So let me ask you a question: When you are with people who are far away from God, do you actually *like* them? You may have the privilege of working with nonbelievers forty hours a week. Do they like you, and you like them? Are people who are far away from God drawn to you because Jesus is in you, and they actually like you? Because this is the only way we can return to seeing the count of followers of Jesus grow innumerably.

Now here's the best part: When we understand the implications of God being for, with, and one of us, that often compels us to invite Jesus to be *in us*. And that changes everything. God himself passes the spiritual DNA of Jesus into our very lives, which empowers us to imitate Jesus' life here on this earth.

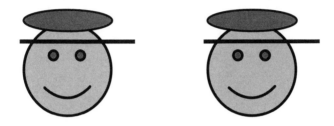

God being for us, with us, and one of us pales in comparison to God being *in us*. We are Jesus' representatives walking around on earth.

So what are the implications of God being for, with, one of, and in us? What does this Christology mean for our lives and the life of the church? Keep in mind that what we believe about Jesus (Christology) determines how we live (missiology), which determines what we do as a church (ecclesiology).

If Jesus is now *in us,* then it follows that, like Jesus, we must be *for* people.

Jesus is in us, and we are now *for* people. But unless they see our lives reflecting the fact that God is for them, they will continue to believe that God is against them. They'll continue to be afraid of God. For us to restore the church to the mission of Jesus, we *must* communicate to people in every way possible that Jesus is *for* them and, therefore, that we as followers of Jesus are *for* them.

Letting Others Know We Are for Them

How should this Christology be lived out by followers of Jesus on mission as the church? In our conversations we must build bridges instead of erecting barriers. In my own family I have found that I don't need to assert "what the Bible says." They have already heard enough of what Christians are telling them the Bible says. It is much more powerful if I actually live like I am *for* them.

I was recently among a gathering of pastors in New York City. I had an evening free and called a friend of mine to see if he could meet me for coffee. This friend of mine is openly homosexual. After coffee, going with him to his favorite bookstore, and walking around the city for a couple of hours, I said to him, "I don't know what to do with your sexuality, but I want you to know that I love you enough to die for you."

And he tearfully replied, "That's enough." My friend knows that I am *for* him.

Not long ago I watched the sunrise from the rooftop of Africa. The climb of Mount Kilimanjaro was by far the most physically strenuous endeavor I had ever attempted. Battling altitude sickness, minus-thirty-degree temperatures, and depleted oxygen, we finally summitted—but not without hardship along the way . . .

At 5:30 AM our guide, Ellee, shouted to me, "Pastor, we are almost there! For the children. For the children." We had decided to use the climb to raise financial resources for children in Tanzania who have been orphaned as a result of the AIDS pandemic.

At 5:45 AM we reached Gilman's Point. At about 18,000 feet, Gilman's is considered the first summit of Kilimanjaro. The vast majority of people stop climbing at this point, so by most standards we had now reached the rooftop of Africa.

The sky began to lighten, and I began to weep. As tears streamed down my face, I tried to wipe them off before they froze. Even though we had reached this first summit, we were still not at the highest point of the mountain. So my tears were more than just a response to the beautiful sunrise!

Ellee explained, "You have done the hardest part. All of you, congratulations! We must hurry to Uhuru Peak. We cannot stay long at this altitude."

Someone asked, "How much longer?"

Ellee's response: "An hour and a half. But it is a gradual climb. Not like what we have just done."

He lied.

After thirty minutes I stopped. I had nothing left. At that altitude it is difficult simply to breathe. I put my weight on my trekking poles and hung my head. Ellee shouted again to me, "Pastor, keep moving! For the children!"

At 7:10 AM we attained the final summit of Kilimanjaro—Uhuru Peak at 19,400 feet. There was little time for celebration. A few quick pictures. Encouraging words. And $54,000 had been raised for the children.

There are many "mountains" that I have watched people climb so that they could be a blessing to others:

- One family completely got out of debt so that they could be more generous with those in need.

- Another family renovated a room in their home so that battered women could stay with them in safety.
- A single mom uses her late-model van to give rides to physically challenged young adults who otherwise would not be able to get to work.

Can I ask you a personal question? When was the last time that you attempted to "climb a mountain" *for* someone who is far away from God? When was the last time that you put your life, reputation, and finances on the line *for* someone because you know that God is for that person?

This reality of God being *for* people plays out in real time by our being *with* people. Not sequestered away in our church buildings or church lives. Just as a reminder, in Matthew 28 Jesus instructed his followers to go into the world and make disciples. Jesus did not tell us to build buildings and invite people to come be like us. But that is exactly what many have been doing. Most Christians would probably concede that God is *for* people, and they might even agree to be *with* people if those people will come and become like them. But according to Jesus the exact opposite is called for—*we* must go and be with people. And I mean really be *with* them.

If we actually enjoy being *with* people, that still may not make people smile (we're changing the way we as Jesus' followers have been perceived in our culture).

Practical Ways to Be with and for Them

Being *with* people means that the church must move outside its walls. It means that we should stop having so many church programs that our people have no time to spend with their unchurched friends. It means that the measures we once used for church success need to change. Instead of counting how many people are "with us," we begin capturing and retelling stories of how the church is "with them."

At RiverTree, the church God has entrusted me to lead, we regularly share stories in our weekend gatherings about how we are *with* people. For our friends Jon and Kelly, this meant sharing the story

> The measures we once used for church success need to change.

of their involvement in the arts community (a community that Christians are notorious for avoiding). Jon is the director of our city's Player's Guild. At one time Jon was cast in the lead role in *Rent* on Broadway. So it seemed like a natural step for Jon to direct the Player's Guild performance of *Rent* here in our city.

Everything was going well until several Christians found out that *Rent* is all about people with differing sexual preferences, drug abuse, and AIDS. Because Jon is a close friend of mine, a few of these well-meaning Christians asked if I would talk to him about the inappropriateness of his involvement with the performance. What they didn't know was that Jon and Kelly were having the entire cast (many of whom were living out *Rent*'s exact lifestyle) over to their house for dinner every Sunday evening. What they didn't know was that *Rent* has an amazing redemptive message. What they didn't know was that those people are exactly who Jesus would be hanging out with if he were here today.

Because Jon was on the crew, he had access into their lives. A trust relationship had been built because Jon was for and with them. If we

unleashed

want people to know that God is *for* them, then we have to be *with* them. But it doesn't stop there.

The only way to really be with people is to become *one of* them. In other words, we may show interest in the same sports teams they like, eat at the same restaurants, hang out at the same coffee shops (or, God forbid, pubs). We authentically live amid people because we understand their hurts, pains, and fears since they are *our* hurts, pains, and fears.

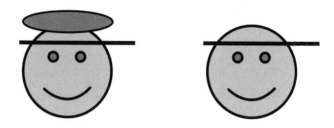

We become like people so that we can become *one of* them.

This *one of* concept has far-reaching implications. I frequently hear people say things like, "Sunday is the most segregated hour of the week." They're referring to the fact that the vast majority of evangelical Christian churches are lily white. Do you know why they're lily white? Because we're not *one of* diverse cultures. Churches composed predominantly of white people build their churches in the suburbs where the community is white like them. They frequent restaurants and parks and shopping malls that are "safe." If we want to see the church become racially diverse, then we must become *one of* people of color. Here are some real practical suggestions:

- Become a Big Brother or a Big Sister to a young person in your community. My wife, Julie, is a Big Sister to a fourteen-year-old girl who lives in the city of Canton, Ohio. This little girl is regularly in our home and my wife is in her home.

- Get your foster care license. In the state of Ohio alone, there are more than fourteen thousand children in the foster care system.[12] My wife and I have been foster parents for the past five years. If you want to begin to build bridges with people of diversity, then invite them into your home. It seems like something Jesus would do.
- Adopt a child. Three years ago, our family adopted our son Elijah. He happens to be a little black boy from Cleveland, Ohio. Today more than 150 families in our church have adopted or are in the process of adopting children. Adopt and see what happens to your heart about "those people."
- Make a move. Move out of your safe, beautiful home in the suburbs and into a home inside the city. Julie and I are currently in the process of selling our home, which sits nestled at the top of three wooded acres, and moving into the city of Canton, recently listed by *Forbes* magazine as the ninth most miserable city in the United States. (Cleveland was number one.)[13] We're not moving because it's a wise financial decision. We're not moving because the schools will be better. We're not moving because we want to live near a cultural center. We're moving because we want to be one of a largely overlooked group of people that Jesus loves deeply.

> We're moving because we want to be one of a largely overlooked group of people that Jesus loves deeply.

Those are just a few of the things that our church is doing. And the good news is that I'm hearing stories just like this from all across the country. As a result, people who are far away from God are starting to get the message: God is *for* them, *with* them, and *one of* them! They are attracted to Jesus, who is now in us; and through the trust relationship we have built by being for, with, and one of them, they in turn will invite

unleashed

Jesus to come live in them. Just like in the book of Acts, the number of disciples will increase daily. Innumerable!

Christlikeness *in us* is transferred to Christlikeness being *in them*.

When we return to the proper order of Christology determining our missiology determining our ecclesiology, we will once again be able to say (like the book of Acts) that the number of people becoming followers of Jesus is *innumerable*!

This renewed understanding of Christology determining missiology determining ecclesiology has transformed the way I read the Gospels. I no longer read them through the lens of American church success, but rather through the lens of what it means to be a servant-spirited follower of Jesus who is interested in bringing God's kingdom now and forever. It has reignited my passion to be a follower of Jesus. I feel closer to the heart of God than at any other time in my ministry. It has transitioned the way I look at and interact with people who are far from God. They are not targets; they are simply people whom Jesus loves—who at any given moment are either moving nearer to or farther away from Jesus. And as a follower of Jesus, I am commissioned to assist them on their journey.

I LOVE THE CHURCH! I continue to believe that it is God's chosen instrument of transformation for our personal lives, for our communities, and ultimately, for the world. I do believe, however, that this transformation will only optimally occur if we understand that what we believe about Jesus must determine our mission, and that will in turn establish how the church functions. This will be evidenced as our lives (both as individuals and together as the church) are lived by being *for* people, *with* people, and *one of* people—who will then respond to Jesus living *in us* by inviting Jesus to live *in them.*

And it is this transforming process that will once again lead us to making disciples of Jesus that are innumerable!

pandemonium

Acts 4:13-22

There has been an absolute explosion of technology in the past decade. Can you even remember not having a cell phone? What was life like before Google and Facebook? What would we do if we couldn't tweet? I can't go back to watching TV in non-HD. I just can't. I live in the age of iPhones and iPods and iPads. I can watch things in 3-D on my 4G laptop connected to my Blu-ray Disc player. Wow.

I really am not a tech guy, and I really don't have a 3-D/4G anything. I'm actually a bit technologically challenged—but I do love teaching from my iPad. It's awesome! For starters, I can make the font as big as I need it (very important at age fifty). Plus it keeps my notes and thoughts in order, even scrolls with a prompter app.

There seems to be an app for just about anything you need. For those of you who aren't reading this book on your Kindle, an app is short for *application*. It's some kind of ingenious program you can download onto your smart phone, iPad, or computer. There are apps for music, spreadsheets, pictures, videos, GPSes, and games. Games like *Angry Birds,* where you go after these pigs who have stolen the birds' eggs and you slingshot the "angry birds" . . . It's addicting and really the best reason to own an iPad.

Causes of Boredom

All this technology has given me a greater appreciation of the Bible. God's Word has contained apps for a long, long time—timeless truth we can apply to our lives that can pretty much address anything that's going on. In fact, my friend Dudley Rutherford is releasing a book called *God Has an App for That*. Because God does. Really. For instance:

- Are you worried? There's an app for that.
- Are you anxious? There's an app for that.
- Are you angry? There's an app for that.
- Got a problem with lust, bitterness, relational friction? There's an app for that.
- Struggling with how to handle your finances? There's an app for that.
- Wanna learn how to really talk to God? There's an app for that.
- Wrestling with an addiction? There's an app for that.
- Bored with your life? There's an app for that too.

Bored? Just what do you find extremely boring? Cleaning the house? Movies with lots of dialogue? What about driving long distances? What about driving long distances to your extended family's house for the holidays? What about sitting in the family room with that extended family all day?

> On those days when the nets sat beside the boat still and empty, you know it had to be boring.

What is it that makes you say, "Man, that bores me out of my mind"? School? Mowing grass? Shoveling snow? Doing your taxes? Watching sports on TV? Watching *anything* on TV? Hunting? Fishing?

Now, I do like to fish—but only when I'm catching something. I'm not a real patient fisherman. I like some action. And when there *is* action, there's nothing any better; but when there's not, there's nothing any more boring than fishing. At least to me.

I'm guessing that at times that's the way *they* felt . . .

Oh, it was an honest, hardworking way to make a living, and sometimes when the nets would fill up with so many fish you couldn't handle them . . . that *had* to be a rush. But on those days when the nets sat beside the boat still and empty, you know it had to be boring.

The Cure for Boredom

And then one day everything changed.

One day as Jesus was walking along the shore of the Sea of Galilee, he saw two brothers—Simon, also called Peter, and Andrew—throwing a net into the water, for they fished for a living. Jesus called out to them, "Come, follow me, and I will show you how to fish for people!" And they left their nets at once and followed him.

A little farther up the shore he saw two other brothers, James and John, sitting in a boat with their father, Zebedee, repairing their nets. And he called them to come, too. They immediately followed him, leaving the boat and their father behind (Matthew 4:18-22, *NLT*).

I once heard someone say, "Boredom is the desire for desires."

Every time the disciples had heard Jesus speak, or when they sat in the boat and had a discussion about the things their friends had heard him say, desire stirred within them.

It was Andrew who first got all stirred up about Jesus. John the Baptist had spoken about Jesus' baptism and the accompanying signs that pointed to him as the Messiah. As Jesus walked by, John shouted, "Look, the Lamb of God, who takes away the sin of the world!" (John 1:29).

The day after this, Andrew and another guy were there with John the Baptist. They ended up hanging out with Jesus all day until around 4:00 PM. The first thing Andrew did was to tell his brother Peter that he had found the Messiah. Word began to spread, and desire began to stir among the fishermen. They didn't know it yet, but their lives were about to move from boredom to pandemonium.

unleashed

Sometimes we forget that these guys could have been young, possibly seventeen to nineteen years old. They were up for a little passion, a little adventure. They definitely had been intrigued and impressed with Jesus for a while. Never had they heard anyone say the kinds of things he said. Never had they heard anyone teach like that. He was nothing like the pious religious leaders they had grown up listening to. The leaders they had been accustomed to had tampered with the pure message of the Scripture. And on top of that, they made following God sound . . . well, boring! But Jesus made it sound like an adventure of faith and passion and purpose. He even said things like, "Unless your righteousness surpasses that of the Pharisees and the teachers of the law, you will certainly not enter the kingdom of heaven" (Matthew 5:20).

I would bet that when Peter heard things like that, he probably thought, *That's the feeling I've always had too! There's got to be more than keeping a bunch of man-made rules. Life has to be more than this. Now I know that I would never be chosen to follow a rabbi. I've been picked over all my life. I know I'm just an unschooled, blue-collar fisherman. But I'm telling you, if I ever got the chance to hang out with a guy like that, I'd do it.*

We don't know exactly how much prior exposure these fishermen had to Jesus, but it was enough to spark their curiosity. Enough to stir some hope in them. Enough to make them dream. Enough to make them lay down their nets and follow him.

Chosen

So let me ask you, "Are you bored?" Well, there's an app for that. Jesus says, "Follow me!" (John 1:43).

If anyone has ever been worthy of being followed, it is Jesus. Even many secular leadership gurus agree that Jesus of Nazareth was an amazing leader. Jesus fleshed out various great leadership principles, but one of the things I most appreciate is the way Jesus was able to see potential in people when no one else did.

Face it, no one would have chosen those fishermen. But Jesus had a way of looking deeper. And still today, he has a way of seeing a person's potential greatness, greatness that a person can't even see in himself.

It's common knowledge that when gold is mined, several tons of dirt are often moved to get an ounce of gold. But no one goes in looking for the dirt; they go in looking for gold. While good leaders certainly don't go in with blinders on, they don't focus solely on people's flaws, imperfections, and blemishes. They try to see what God sees in a person. They look deeper for the "gold." They try to imagine what that person could become. I want that set of eyes, don't you?

Have you ever browsed through a clearance rack and seen the label "slightly imperfect"? Unless there is a huge hole in the front of a shirt or something, we usually find that we're getting a pretty good deal. But when it comes to choosing people, we have a tendency to look for—and expect—a flawless specimen.

Have you ever said (or thought) something like this:

- "She's really nice. She's cute and kind, and she loves God. But I don't know about dating her. Her laugh is kind of goofy."
- "He's a super nice guy, has a wonderful personality. He's funny and has a great heart, but I'm looking for a guy with really tight abs."
- "Yeah, I know my kid is a terrific kid, but he's so terrible at soccer."
- "Oh, I know she got four As, but that one B . . ."
- "My husband is an awesome dad, he's warm and friendly, he's even romantic. I just wish he made more money."
- "Yeah, my wife is a great mom and a wonderful friend, but since she's put on all that weight . . ."

unleashed

Listen, we're *all* slightly imperfect. We're *all* clearance rack material! We've got to learn to look at each other through the eyes of Jesus, who sees great potential in all of us.

God has always seen more than meets the eye.

- Moses stuttered.
- David was too young.
- Abraham was too old.
- Solomon was too rich.
- Naomi was too poor.
- Jonah ran from God.
- Noah got drunk.
- Timothy got ulcers.
- Rahab was a prostitute.
- Gideon doubted.
- Elijah burned out.
- Martha worried too much.
- Peter bragged too much.
- John the Baptist was just flat-out weird!

> We've got to learn to look at each other through the eyes of Jesus, who sees great potential in all of us.

But God saw potential in them that no one else saw, and he used their lives for eternal purposes. Man, if I could only learn to look at others the way Jesus looks at them!

Can you imagine how those first disciples felt when Jesus chose them? Essentially, he drafted them as "lottery picks."

"Long before he laid down the earth's foundations, he had *us* in mind, had settled on *us* as the focus of his love, to be made whole and holy by his love. Long, long ago he decided to adopt *us* into his family through Jesus Christ. (What pleasure he took in planning this!) He wanted *us* to enter into the celebration of his lavish gift-giving by the hand of his beloved Son" (Ephesians 1:4-6, *The Message*, emphasis added).

Man, what a feeling to be chosen. To hear our Creator whisper to ragged, picked-over people like us, "I love you. I choose you. I've always wanted you to be my son, my daughter. Follow me."

> *They must believe I could help make this team/ this company/this ministry/ this family better. They want me. They chose me.*

When you are chosen it makes you feel like a contributor, like a player, doesn't it? You begin to think, *They really want what I can bring. They actually think I could add some value here. They must believe I could help make this team/this company/ this ministry/this family better. They want me. They chose me.*

When I am chosen, it means somebody wants me. I am desired. I am loved. I belong. But whether other *people* choose me or not—and regardless of my past and my imperfections—somebody wants me! And that same Somebody wants you. You are the focus of his love. He sees amazing potential in you!

Look what it says in 1 Peter 2:9: "You are the ones *chosen* by God, *chosen* for the high calling of priestly work, *chosen* to be a holy people, God's instruments to do his work and speak out for him, to tell others of the night-and-day difference he made for you—from nothing to something, from rejected to accepted" (*The Message,* emphasis added).

Did you notice who wrote that? A former fisherman! A guy who was chosen. A guy who moved from boredom to pandemonium in ways

unleashed

he never dreamed he would. All because this great leader, Jesus, saw potential in him, chose him, and instilled in him that he had something meaningful to contribute.

Every one of the disciples knew they had been chosen by Jesus. They just had no way of knowing the magnitude of that choice. They had no idea the adventures they would be a part of. They never imagined the mouth-dropping, awe-inspiring things they would see and hear, write about, and speak about. They had no idea the countless lives their lives would touch. They had no idea the pandemonium they would cause. They just knew they were desired. Jesus said, "Follow me." And they did.

Pandemonium Breaks Loose

I don't believe that when the fishermen left their nets that day to follow Jesus, they ever imagined what would unfold three years later. Never in their wildest dreams did they see themselves standing up in front of people, preaching and teaching. I'm guessing they never thought, *Hey, if we follow this guy, maybe someday we'll be able to heal people too.*

But that's exactly what happened.

One afternoon (you can read about it in Acts 3) Peter and John were heading up to the temple for the 3:00 PM prayer time. Tons of people did this every day. On their way in, a beggar who had been disabled since birth asked them for some cash. They had been learning to look deeper at people (hanging out with Jesus will do that to you), and they saw that what the beggar really needed was some hope and a touch from God. So they looked straight at the man and said, "We're a little short on cash, but we'll give you what else we got. In the name of Jesus the Messiah from Nazareth, get up and walk" (see v. 6).

The guy instantly received healing and began doing the moonwalk, the Dougie, the jitterbug . . . (insert your own *Dancing with the Stars* dance of choice)—and praised God for the first steps he'd ever taken! When the people saw this person they recognized as "that disabled, homeless guy who begs every day by the gate" now up and running around, pandemonium broke out. Huge crowds gathered to hear from Peter and John.

Peter preached a passion-filled, history-filled, truth-filled, grace-filled, hope-filled message on the front porch of the temple; and it created quite a stir. In fact, thousands of people became followers of Jesus that day!

> Peter preached a passion-filled, history-filled, truth-filled, grace-filled, hope-filled message on the front porch of the temple.

Well, the religious leaders (the same ones who'd handed Jesus over to be executed) pushed their way through the crowd and had Peter and John arrested and thrown in jail. The next day the religious teachers of the law ran Peter and John through an interrogation process and asked them point-blank, "By what power or what name did you do this?" (Acts 4:7).

Filled with the Holy Spirit, Peter responded:

> Are we being questioned today because we've done a good deed for a crippled man? Do you want to know how he was healed? Let me clearly state to all of you and to all the people of Israel that he was healed by the powerful name of Jesus Christ the Nazarene, the man you crucified but whom God raised from the dead. For Jesus is the one referred to in the Scriptures, where it says, "The stone that you builders rejected has now become the cornerstone."
>
> There is salvation in no one else! God has given no other name under heaven by which we must be saved (vv. 9-12, NLT).

unleashed

Check out the reaction: "When they saw the courage of Peter and John and realized that they were unschooled, ordinary men, they were astonished and they took note that these men had been with Jesus" (v. 13).

I think that's one of the coolest passages in Scripture. They took note that these men had been with Jesus. No other explanation for this kind of passion. No other explanation for this kind of confidence. No other explanation for this kind of courage. The only reason this much purpose was surging through these guys' veins was that Jesus had said, "Follow me" . . . and they did!

We Cannot Help It!

Just think about this. If we will imitate what the disciples did—by spending time "with Jesus" in the Word and in prayer—we will also be empowered for whatever situations into which God might unleash us!

Look again at Acts 4. The leaders "called the apostles back in and commanded them never again to speak or teach in the name of Jesus. But Peter and John replied, 'Do you think God wants us to obey you rather than him? We cannot stop telling about everything we have seen and heard'" (vv. 18-20, *NLT*).

> Our lives were so empty, much like yours (well, maybe not *that* empty).

In other words, "We're sorry, but sirs, you don't understand. Three years ago we were fixing our nets. We were bored out of our minds. We knew there had to be so much more than following man-made rules. Our lives were so empty, much like yours (well, maybe not *that* empty), but then he walked by our boat and said 'Follow me,' and everything changed! We can't shut up about the things we've seen him do. We can't stop talking about the things we've heard him say. He alone has the words of life. He alone holds the keys to deep satisfaction. He alone breathes life into empty people like us. He alone can forgive someone like me . . . and you guys, for that matter. He is the one who, if you let him, will take you places you never dreamed you'd go. He will lead you on adventures that you never, ever saw yourself taking. You see, following him is our life! Man, I wish you knew him too. We're sorry, but we just *can't* shut up about him!"

Verses 21, 22 say that the council threatened them further but had to let them go. They couldn't figure out a way to keep sheer pandemonium from breaking out among the people, because the people knew they had witnessed the greatness of God in their midst.

As I was rereading this story, I got to thinking, *Wonder what those two young guys said to each other as they walked out the door?* Maybe . . .

"John, dude, can you believe what just happened?!"

"I know! Pete, when that guy asked us for cash, and we both sensed that God was speaking to us, 'Go ahead, you have my power in you. Heal the guy' . . . Was that scary or what? I know all the people around heard you tell him to get up in the name of Jesus— because your voice carries, Pete. What if the guy had just stayed there? Do you know how stupid we would've looked?"

"Yeah, but he didn't, did he! [*they exchange high fives and chest bumps*] This is simply unbelievable! This is awesome! Did you see all those people give their lives to follow Jesus?"

"Yeah, we are *catching* people, just like he said we would! Did you ever think in a million years that the two of us would get to do something like this?!"

Can I ask you again, "Are you bored?" There's an app for that: follow him.

Maybe right now your life is missing that sense of adventure. If truth were told, you are not passionate about much these days. Really. I look around and see so many people who are bored out of their minds. There's no passion, no all-consuming purpose. They are stuck in the same ol' routine every day. They have no interest in creating anything even resembling pandemonium. Just keep it calm, comfortable, and risk free.

If their lives were a flavor of ice cream, it would be the flavor *beige*.

I've talked for years about how some people get into a swimming pool. Many are "toe dippers." They just stick in a toe and cringe at how cold the water is. Then they wade in ankle deep. "Oooh!" Then calves—"Oooh!" Knees—"Oooh!" Thighs—"Oooh!" Oh man, that's such a miserable way to get into a pool.

How *do* you get into a pool? Yeah, you take a running start and tuck your knees to your chest and do a cannonball! You hit the water, and the water goes flying everywhere. The ripples go out and hit the sides of the pool. And they go back in and back out, back in and back out, and if you're really big they go back in . . ." If the sides of the pool weren't there, the ripples would keep on going long after you made your splash.

> Jesus calls his church to make some ripples, ripples that will be felt long after we're gone.

I believe that's what God calls us to do with our lives. That's what it means to follow Jesus. To jump in with reckless abandon and create some ripples. To touch a life that will touch a life that will touch a life . . . to create some positive pandemonium that will touch people in eternal ways!

Jesus calls his church to make some ripples, ripples that will be felt long after we're gone. He calls us to stir up some hope. To confront culture with grace and the truth of God's Word in compassion and authenticity.

Do you remember what was said about the first-century followers of Jesus? They were the men and women who turned the world upside down by following Jesus with reckless abandon. It seems like everywhere they went, they created pandemonium. They were always stirring up hope. They were always making some ripples.

And we're still feeling those ripples today.

Anything But Boring

I think back to all the times I refused to follow—I mean, really follow—Jesus, and I wonder what I've missed. I have few regrets in life, but all of them center around not saying yes to the leadership of

> I have few regrets in life, but all of them center around not saying yes to the leadership of God.

God. All of them concern ignoring the promptings of the Holy Spirit. All of them deal with not having the courage to actually walk by faith.

And the reason I wonder what I've missed is because I *have* experienced the thrill of following him. I have said yes many, many times. And I have followed him enough to know that when you follow—really follow—he will take you to places you never could have imagined going. You'll go down paths you never even knew existed. Your life will intersect with people whose lives will change yours. From my personal life experience I know that following Jesus—really following Jesus—is anything but boring!

I think of some friends of mine who are following Jesus and, thus, creating a little positive pandemonium with their lives.

My friend Thomas is a brilliant twenty-five-year-old. He graduated from Duke University with a degree in computer science/finance and a minor in Russian. Told you he was smart! A corporation in Dallas thought so too, and hired him right out of school. I mean, the guy is a catch, a budding superstar.

unleashed

He began to attend a church where he met a couple who were working in the Sudan. They had been trying to figure out how to really help poor people find a better life, and began to ask my friend about micro-financing. Well, to make a long story short, Thomas decided to follow Jesus' lead. He quit his job and his climb up the corporate ladder and now lives in the Sudan, making loans to poor people and teaching them about Jesus.

His ministry might give a $100 loan to someone who wants to start a business but has never had the opportunity. They may buy one sewing machine to start a seamstress shop, make some money to buy another one, then pay back the loan. And that money gets passed along to another poor entrepreneur. Kind of like making ripples.

You could use a lot of words to describe his life, but *boring* would not be one of them.

Thomas lives in a war-torn country in a concrete-block room with no AC. He rides an old dirt bike everywhere he goes—has had three wrecks on it. But he's never been more fully alive than he is right now. He is filled with a sense of purpose and joy. You could use a lot of words to describe his life, but *boring* would not be one of them.

I'm thinking about Marilyn, who for years has been following Jesus by taking in terminally ill foster kids. She loves them for as long as they have left so that they will walk into eternity knowing the Lord who made Heaven possible. Expensive. Exhausting. Deeply satisfying. Grace-filled. Anything but boring.

I held the funeral for a high school friend named Bud. He was murdered. Like Peter and John, he was a fisherman. Not a fisherman by trade, just by passion—he loved to be out on the water. Bud was a simple, hard-working guy. He was one of those people who was loved by everybody and about whom you'd think, *He doesn't have an enemy in this world.*

But apparently he did.

A man Bud had had to fire about three years before had been holding a grudge the whole time. That unresolved resentment and bitterness gave way to distorted thinking. Add alcohol. And one night, out of the blue, he walked into Bud's house and shot him three times in the chest. Tragic for both.

I spent some time with Bud's eighty-year-old dad. With tears streaming down his face, he said, "Bud was just the best. He would stop by every day to check on his mother and me. We don't get around like we used to, so he would bring us groceries and would fix anything that needed fixing. He was such a good boy."

> Look for opportunities to live beyond yourself, for ways to follow Jesus into adventures of touching someone else's life.

I know some would see taking care of your aging parents as a boring "have to." Not Bud. For him it was a "get to" adventure of living beyond himself every day. It was one of the ways he simply followed Jesus.

Every time you live beyond yourself, every time you roll up your sleeves and serve people in Jesus' name, your life is anything but boring.

Your job might be one of those routine, same old same old kind of jobs, but it doesn't have to be. Start showing up at work with a sense of God's presence. Look for opportunities to live beyond yourself, for ways to follow Jesus into adventures of touching someone else's life.

Before you head off to school, roll out of bed and pray, "God, lead me today. Put someone in my path who needs a touch from you. I will listen and follow. I want to create some positive pandemonium in my school."

I love the way *The Message* puts Romans 12:1: "So here's what I want you to do, God helping you: Take your everyday, ordinary life—your

unleashed

sleeping, eating, going-to-work, and walking-around life—and place it before God as an offering. Embracing what God does for you is the best thing you can do for him."

It seems to me that more and more churches all over the world, both large and small, are stirring up hope these days. I happen to be a part of a couple of churches that are trying to do just that. Southland Christian Church has been causing pandemonium in the city of Lexington, Kentucky, for over fifty years now. Built on a foundation of love and other-centered living motivated by an obedience to God's Word, the church has all kinds of ministries bringing help and hope to the city and beyond. Clothing, food, mentoring for public school kids, addiction help, proms for special-needs people, free medical clinics for uninsured people, a refuge for women wanting to get out of the adult entertainment business, and on and on and on. As a result of the members following Jesus' commands, the people they serve want to know about Jesus.

> As a result of the members following Jesus' commands, the people they serve want to know about Jesus.

Heartland Community Church in Rockford, Illinois, is also a place full of people committed to making ripples with their lives. It is a bunch of real and raw, grateful-for-a-second-chance, changed-by-grace folks who are stirring up hope, creating some pandemonium in the city. Rockford is a tough place with a really high unemployment rate, high crime, racial unrest, and a severely struggling public school system. We felt like Jesus was saying, "Come on, follow me into these schools. Bring some help and hope." And that's what we've been trying to do.

Thousands of people donate their vacation time and cash to help refurbish these old schools, where 92 percent of the kids live at or below the poverty level. This outreach we felt compelled to start is called

unleashed

Sharefest. We have now linked arms with churches, businesses, students, faculty . . . and a whole community is trying to make a difference together. There is no mistaking that Jesus is the reason we're doing it, and that has created some pandemonium in the city. Positive pandemonium. Ripples.

When Heartland decided to take on the task of packing a million meals for earthquake victims in Haiti, the public school system called and asked if they could help. All five public high schools dismissed students from classes so they could pack meals. Junior high students collected "Quarters for the Quake" and brought them to Heartland. We pooled our resources and packed a million meals and sent them to Northwest Haiti Christian Mission. No one screamed "Separation of church and state!" Just people together trying to make some ripples. Just a church trying to follow Jesus.

Chasing the Goose

In his book *Wild Goose Chase,* Mark Batterson writes about how the Celtic Christians had a unique name for the Holy Spirit: *"An Geadh-Glas,"* or "the Wild Goose." They saw God's Spirit as someone who could not "be tracked or tamed. An element of danger, an air of unpredictability" were surrounding him.[1]

Mark Batterson talks about having what he calls an "inverted relationship with God": "Instead of following the Spirit, we invite the Spirit to follow us. Instead of serving God's purposes, we want Him to serve our purposes. And while this may seem like a subtle distinction, it makes an ocean of difference. The result of this inverted relationship with God is not just a self-absorbed spirituality that leaves us feeling empty, it's also the difference between spiritual boredom and spiritual adventure."[2]

I'm learning that if you chase the Wild Goose, he will take you places you never could have imagined going. You'll go down paths you never even knew existed. It's a chase that will be anything but boring!

unleashed

I've been trying to follow him since I was seventeen years old. Up until then I just *went to church*. Big difference. I surrendered my life to Jesus on the banks of a lake in northern Minnesota. I will never forget it. I put my hands in the air. I'd never done that in my life. In the church I grew up in, if you raised your hand the response would be, "Do you have a question?" So raising my hands was not something I practiced regularly, but instinctively, as a broken teenage guy, I lifted them up as an act of surrender and—to be honest—exhaustion. I was tired of doing life on my own and faking a relationship with God. That night I asked Jesus to forgive me, and I told him that I would go wherever he wanted me to go. Little did I know what all that would mean.

> That night I asked Jesus to forgive me, and I told him that I would go wherever he wanted me to go. Little did I know what all that would mean.

My wife, Debbie, and I have had seventeen different addresses since we've been married. Some of those involved flipping houses, but most involved a ministry move. I know that's a shocker! You would look at my résumé (if I had one) and say, "Man, that dude can't keep a job!"

Well, maybe not, but every move we've made really did seem like a Wild Goose chase, so to speak. It has simply felt like following through on what I said as a seventeen-year-old: "Wherever your Spirit leads, I'll follow."

I cringe when I think of how many times I've probably missed or even intentionally ignored the promptings of the Holy Spirit. But I celebrate the adventures that all the "Yes, I'll do that" promises have led to.

I am from Lexington, Kentucky. Born and raised there. I love the place. So when I got the opportunity to do ministry there in my hometown, I was blown away. We had been leading a church-plant team in

Las Vegas and having the time of our lives, but God asked us to move to Lexington and help a church through transition. It ripped our hearts out to leave Vegas and our team and friends there, but we knew we were supposed to go.

Leading a church through transition is extremely challenging, and it certainly keeps you on your knees. You learn a lot about yourself, about other people, about human nature—and you learn a lot of leadership lessons. It's not easy. But I also felt the hand of God on my life and felt his power flowing through me. It was one of those adventures when you get to see God supernaturally moving in the lives of people every day. It was a blast.

We were doing life with all our family around. We had great friends and served on a great team—at a church that was causing some pandemonium, making a difference in the city and in the world. And I really thought this would be the last stop on the ministry train.

Not so.

I won't take the time to explain all the inner workings and promptings and circumstances that took place, but we thought God was

> We had great friends and served on a great team—at a church that was causing some pandemonium, making a difference in the city and in the world.

asking us to pack up and accept a new challenge in Chicago. I didn't understand it all, but knew in my soul that he was asking me to go. So I resigned from a church I loved with all my heart, left our family and friends, and headed north to a cold, windy city.

The day after I announced to the Southland church that I was leaving, I was sitting in the airport, waiting to board a flight to Chicago. Ever have buyer remorse? Ever have that feeling about God? "God, did I hear you right, or was it just the pepperoni talking?" You know what I mean, right?

unleashed

I was so down about the whole thing as I sat there by myself at gate C2 thinking, *What have I done? This really stinks.* I was reading *USA Today* when this guy plopped down in the seat next to me and asked, "Any good news?"

I smiled and said, "Not much."

He asked, "Where you headed?"

"Chicago. How 'bout you?"

"Oslo, Norway. I connect through Chicago, but I'm going to Oslo to pray for three days. I work in the horse industry. [*Lexington is the horse farm capital of the world.*] I'm kind of a chaplain for folks who work in the barns and paddocks of racetracks. A lot of them have had a rough life and need a touch from God. Oslo has a racing presence, and I think God is asking me to go over there and pray for an opportunity to open up so I can start a ministry there. I don't know if you are a Christian or not, but I just try to go wherever God is leading me."

"Uh-huh."

As I continued to read the sports section, he rambled on and on about what he was doing and what he was praying about, until we boarded the plane. He sat just one seat behind me, across the aisle.

As we were making our final descent into O'Hare, my newfound Oslo friend reached up, grabbed my arm, and said, "Hey, I don't know who you are or why you're going to Chicago, but I just had a vision about you."

I was thinking, *Oh great, this whacked-out Norwegian horse guy interprets dreams.* Cynicism was now walking hand in hand with my depression.

He continued, "I saw you standing behind an old-fashioned water pump with your hand on the handle and thousands of people lined up with empty cups. Again, I don't know who you are, but I thought I needed to tell you that. You can take it for what it's worth."

Well, I got goose bumps (make that Wild Goose bumps) all over my body. And in that moment I could sense God saying to me, "Come on, just trust me. It's going to be OK. There are millions of thirsty people just waiting for you to serve up some living water. When you were seventeen you said, 'Wherever.' Remember that? Just keep following me. I love you and want to use you."

My daughter snapped a photograph I have hanging in my office. Wanna guess what it is? It is an old water pump. It reminds me of all the thirsty people in this world who have yet to be reached. It also helps me to live in the awareness of God's presence in my life. And it reminds me to listen and follow his promptings every day—even when they don't make a lot of sense in the moment. Daily I have to remind myself that he is a lot better at leading me than I am.

> It reminds me to listen and follow his promptings every day—even when they don't make a lot of sense in the moment.

So let me ask you again, "Are you bored?" There's an app for that: follow him.

You want a life filled with adventure? Then follow him. Want to experience life to the full? Then follow him. Want to be a better husband? Want to be a better mom? Then follow him. What to be a better friend? Want to experience the thrill of being used by God to touch people's lives? Then follow him. Want to know power? Want to know deep satisfaction every day? Want to make some ripples? Want to be a part of a movement that is causing some pandemonium and stirring up hope?

Then follow him.

Really follow him.

shaken

Acts 4:23-31

I am the oldest of three siblings. I learned at a very young age that if I was going to have two younger sisters in my life—moving me out of the "cute little one" position—I would have to utilize them to my advantage (I say that with a huge smile on my face). I would ask my parents or grandparents for snacks all the time, and often they would tell me no. I would then call the "team" together and persuade my youngest sister to go and ask for snacks for *us*. After all, who could say no to that cute little face?

My parents quickly caught on to my ploy, and what worked a few times eventually ran its course. Not to be outsmarted, my next move was to go to my parents with *both* my younger sisters, and together we would ask for the snacks. That began to work more frequently. Out of three pairs of eyes, at least one pair was bound to soften our parents.

Here's the life lesson I learned: when a group comes together and makes its request to a person in authority, the group is more likely to receive a favorable response. Instead of going solo, there is something much more powerful about coming together as one to solicit a response from the person in charge.

I believe this is also true in our relationship with God. He desires to respond powerfully to his people, especially when they come together as one body, one mind, and one spirit making their requests known to him.

I am part of a body of believers at Shepherd of the Hills Church who come from diverse cultural backgrounds but gather together in one place, worshipping one God—and this is a testimony to what a powerful God we serve. It is a privilege to be connected to the greatest source of power in the world, the God of the universe, and to the name that makes even the demons in the spiritual realm quiver and flee— Jesus. Sometimes we forget that we have daily access to this power, in the midst of watching the rapid advancement of evil in this world. It is an evil whose perversion is outpacing the advancement of technology and progressing at a greater rate than medical breakthroughs. It is an evil that is creatively convincing the world of its validity and, in some cases, its necessity. Yes, it is absolutely mind-blowing to know that we still have daily access to a power that will crush this evil.

God's desire is to shake up this Babylonia-like world. He vigilantly pursues his creation to restore what once was whole. God can do whatever he so chooses to restore order, and he has chosen to release the power of the kingdom through his church, the body of Christ, today. And so I pose this question: Do you think at this point in history, and specifically in your life, that the kingdom of God is advancing as rapidly and powerfully as it should be, when compared with the frantic progress of the kingdom of our enemy? Who's outpacing whom? The church is held accountable for its participation in shaking up the world.

Before going any further, I believe we need to honestly do an inventory of what we truly want from God in our lives and through our lives as his vessels. Do you want God to shake up your family? your marriage? your relationships? your career? Because we are creatures of comfort by nature, we surely desire comfort more than we welcome things being shaken up. *Comfort* implies convenience, complacency, easy living, and tranquility; every day as a "riding off into the beautiful sunset" moment. Conversely, *shaken* suggests inconvenience, change, unknown—something we are not used to. It would seem only right to believe that when God decides to move, comfort would be thrown out the window.

Can we say that's what we really want? I believe that God wants to shake things up because he doesn't want us to become too comfortable; that's where apathy becomes part of our being. Other than the fact that God was *with* them, there was nothing complacent and comfortable about the lives of Jesus and his disciples. Remember, he did not promise that life would be comfortable. As a matter of fact, he said, "Everyone will hate you because of me" (Luke 21:17).

If we are committed followers of Jesus, there are a few things we must embrace when asking God to stir up our lives and the lives of those around us. We should expect and welcome the unknown. We must welcome unity, for unity is certainly in the heart of God. It is expressed in his oneness as the Father, the Son, and the Spirit. And we must welcome persecution. God allows persecution against the church to move her away from apathy and to provide opportunities to advance his kingdom.

> God decided he wanted to ignite his church and shake up the very ground it stood on.

Not long after the church was founded on the Day of Pentecost, God decided he wanted to ignite his church and shake up the very ground it stood on. There is a fascinating account of this in Acts 4:23-31.

Unity Excites the Spirit of God

As I walked out of a ballroom where I had just spoken to a group of men of all ages, backgrounds, and levels of spiritual maturity, a Caucasian man, possibly in his fifties, approached me in the hallway. He began to share with me how that morning was the first time he had ever heard a black man speak in person. He went on to explain how he grew up in an area of Texas where there weren't many, if any, African-Americans. It was an area where racism was common; prejudice was the norm. He continued to tell me that he grew up in a racist family, and racism was all he knew. After hearing the message that God spoke through me, he admitted that the Holy Spirit was dealing with his heart, and he was glad that God used me to preach a word that touched his heart. He reached to embrace me in appreciation for the message. I returned his hug and thanked him for his encouragement, transparency, and honesty.

I know that God was excited at that moment when a line of division, based on race, was torn down by the Spirit and the Word of God. Otherwise, how could two men worship together if one had a dislike toward the other, or a bias against the other, based on anything—especially race?

Together

In Acts 4 Peter and John had been brought out of prison—having been arrested for preaching the resurrection of Jesus (v. 2)—but they were still being interrogated by a council of elders, rulers, and teachers of the law in connection with performing a miraculous deed for a disabled man. When Peter and John were released after being threatened, they returned to their friends, and *together* they lifted their voices to the Lord (v. 24). The emphasis here is on *together*. There is a theme in Scripture that reveals the heart of God and how the Spirit of God becomes excited and is invited to move among believers who walk together in agreement. In Acts 2:1 the apostles were all together in one place, waiting obediently for the promise of the Holy Spirit—as Jesus had told them to do. Their waiting was a type of invitation for the Spirit not only to lead them where Jesus wanted them to go but also to fill them as well. After Peter's passionate sermon about the gospel on the Day of

> Their waiting was a type of invitation for the Spirit not only to lead them where Jesus wanted them to go but also to fill them as well.

Pentecost, we see this repetition of the believers joined together, devoted to the fellowship (v. 42); meeting together and having all things in common (v. 44); and meeting together for the purpose of sharing meals and Communion as one (v. 46).

In John 17:21-23, three times Jesus prayed for believers to be one as he and the Father are one, that they be perfected in unity. In Ephesians 4:3 Paul described what it means to walk in a manner worthy of the calling—to "keep the unity of the Spirit through the bond of peace." The reason we ought to do so is because "there is one body and one Spirit, just as you were called to one hope" (v. 4). My friends, this is not exclusive to one particular part of the body of Christ. This is a call for all of us to honor.

God is seriously concerned about unity and oneness in the body of Christ. It is a picture of the intimate yet powerful relationship between God and his Son, as well as an equally powerful relationship between God and the church. When the Holy Spirit is invited to dwell among a group of believers who are united, God becomes excited to move in power.

Different, But One

Have you noticed how some professional athletes exhibit selfishness because of their entitlement issues? Have you ever known a group of singers in which individuals with diva issues desired to command the stage with their lead vocals, to the detriment of the whole choir? If we're not careful, the church can revert to being as selfish and entitled as the pagan world—devoid of the unifying and indwelling Spirit of God. Sometimes we're guilty of coveting the glamour of spiritual gifts and the glory they may bring when we use them. We move in isolation and self-sufficiency or in cliques (often sugarcoated or masked by being called affinity groups). The root of these problems is often fragile egos yearning for a steroid shot of esteem—and this spirit is a cancer that divides. It

unleashed

can send us in many divisive directions, just as denominations have been experiencing for many years.

In contrast, there is nothing more powerful than a team of athletes, a choir of singers, or the members of Christ's body—the church—who are all on the same page. We must be on our guard. The enemy lies in wait, asking permission to sift us like wheat (Luke 22:31). Whatever is God's priority to sustain will be the enemy's mission to dismantle, and vice versa; whatever is a mission for the enemy will be important for God to crush. If Satan is vigilant about division and isolation, then God is just as vigilant about unity in the church. I believe it excites the Spirit of God when we are one. It is in this oneness that we find the miracle of healing, when we confess to our brothers our sins so that we might be healed (James 5:16). It is in this oneness that we find peace, intimacy, and power.

> There is nothing more powerful than a team of athletes, a choir of singers, or the members of Christ's body—the church—who are all on the same page.

What might Satan be using to divide our homes, our relationships, our ministries, our churches? Disunity is where the enemy flourishes. A helpful question to ask yourself is: *Is Satan flourishing or prospering in my life more than God is?*

Why do we have such a propensity to be disunited on so many fronts? There are several reasons why, but perhaps the most important of those reasons is that none of us is exactly alike. We are all designed uniquely—from our gender, personalities, and giftedness to our cultural, ethnic, and generational perspectives. We are all different.

Unfortunately, too many of us are afraid of whatever is different from ourselves. We are scared of the unknown. We mark it as if to blacklist something that fits a particular description of whatever is unlike us. So we form—and settle for unity within—our "affinity groups" that are safe and comfortable. There is a spirit that comes with this mind-set, and it says to anyone who doesn't think, speak, dress, or act like our group: "Do not enter" or "Lot full!"

On the other hand, true unity introduces us to diversity. When we think with an attitude that encourages diversity, we welcome the unknown, no matter how scary. It challenges us, exposes the ugly in us, and reveals our strengths and weaknesses, because of the strengths and weaknesses brought to the table by those who are not like us. Unity in the body embraces the *unknown* so that together we can embrace the God we *know* in the kind of worship that excites the Spirit of God—"in the Spirit and in truth" (John 4:24). If you dare, ask yourself these questions:

> Unity in the body embraces the *unknown* so that together we can embrace the God we *know* in worship.

- Am I willing to welcome the unknown on my church campus *and* at my front door?
- Can I pray with, serve with, and break bread with the unknowns in the body of Christ around me?
- Does that embrace go beyond Sundays, life groups, and midweek Bible studies?

The mutual love of the believers is how nonbelievers will know we are disciples of Jesus (John 13:35), because love is the greatest bond of unity that we know.

Unleashed from Bondage

Remember the man I mentioned earlier whom I met in the hallway outside the ballroom where I was speaking? What I did not share with you was why the experience was so significant to me.

I am a country boy from South Carolina who experienced firsthand, in-your-face, blatant racism. I know what it looks like when it takes a more subtle form, but with the same hatred and same hurt. My family has dealt with and indirectly still deals with the residuals of bitter hatred toward black folks. It is said, but not officially recorded by the law, that my grandfather was killed by racist, white people in the mid 1950s. This happened when my father was just two years old. He found out when he was nine and has been a very angry, oftentimes violent man ever since. He is nearing the age of sixty and is not the same violent man he was thirty years ago. But the truth of his father's unjust death led him to live this life apart from his biological father with anger in his heart—and narcotics and alcohol in his system. (Praise God, he has finally been delivered!)

That was the father that my sisters and I saw the most—an angry, quick-tempered, and often absent man. Even though my sisters and I are adults now, I can still see evidence of our trying to undo the damage caused by a broken household and tenuous relationship with our father. Not only did I not get to know my grandfather, but I had to deal with the spiritual, emotional, and mostly physical absence of my own dad. I could easily have carried that same hatred and anger toward white people in my heart just as my father did, but God's grace would not allow that to happen, even in my younger days when I experienced bigotry and wanted to hate.

A white man, who grew up with racism ingrained in his mind, embracing a young black man, who never met his grandfather because of racism, is a miracle. Two men from different races, cultures, and even generations—but who share the same faith—came together and would not allow the enemy the opportunity to discourage either of them from expressing love and appreciation for the other. The white man I encountered that day does not know to this day the testimony I just shared. Inside I was fighting to hold back tears of joy because I knew all that God had done over the years with my own heart—both leading up to the moment and also allowing it to happen. I know the Spirit of God is excited because I can feel the stirring of his excitement inside me. This is what can happen everywhere when the Spirit of God is unleashed to shake up lives for his glory!

Persecution Incites the Spirit of God

It seems to me like the greatest oxymoron related to Christianity is *Christian persecution.* Why would there be so much attack against the people who are supposed to be protected by Almighty God? Here's one possible reason why persecution comes our way: if there were no trials, attacks, and persecution, then we would become more and more dependent on ourselves rather than God. That is just our nature. Another benefit of persecution is that it incites the Spirit of God to move through and on behalf of believers.

> Why would there be so much attack against the people who are supposed to be protected by Almighty God?

To *incite* means to encourage or stir up to act, most times even violently. It is that type of stirred response that the church needs in reaction to persecution—a violence. Not the out-of-control kind, but violence as a great force without fear and regard of safety and comfort for self. The reason? We must match the intensity of the warfare that comes against us. I am not saying that we fight the same way the world does, but that we match the effort it takes to endure in the battle and advance the kingdom of God. Persecution against his followers incites the Spirit of God to move with power and intensity.

Kobe Bryant is arguably one of the best basketball players in the NBA right now, whether you like him or not. That is why opposing teams double- and triple-team him with regularity. In basketball

unleashed

terminology that means there are two or three people guarding one player. Opposing teams try to foul him a little harder and make it more difficult for him, in hopes that his team will not have as good a chance to win the game and, ultimately, the championship. If Kobe were merely an average ballplayer, teams would not pay as much attention to him, and he would oftentimes go undetected, under the radar of the opponent's game plan. Because he is a great player, he takes the most hits, he must concentrate the hardest, and he aggressively leads by example in all phases of the game. His opponents incite him to assert himself. Kobe Bryant endures the blame more than anyone else when his team, the Los Angeles Lakers, loses. Of course, when they win he receives the credit as well. Because of the attention he receives from the other teams, he must depend on his coach's expertise and preparation and on his teammates for support. It would be a mistake to try to do it all alone, burn himself out, and ultimately lose.

> They continued to ask God to consider the threats coming against those who were following his Son and to protect and move on their behalf.

Jesus is the narrow path to the Father. Those who follow him must endure the most and depend the most on the perfect will of the Father, so that they might live. Our winning comes in the form of abundant life here and now, and receiving the inheritance of Heaven for eternity.

Look again at Acts 4. In their prayers, Peter and John recalled David prophetically speaking about the kings on the earth who gathered together and conspired against him, and in doing so conspired against God (vv. 23-26). What they recalled in their prayer was exactly what was also happening to them at that time. They mentioned Herod, Pontius Pilate, the Gentiles, and the people of Israel all coming against God's servant, his anointed one, Jesus (v. 27). They continued to ask God to consider the threats coming against those who were following his Son and to protect and move on their behalf.

Embracing Persecution

It is interesting to note that persecution is what inspired this prayer, to which God responded by shaking up the place. Peter and John were just out of prison; and at the interrogating hands of Jewish leaders, they had been asked not to speak anymore in the name of Jesus. They were specifically targeted because of their faith and proclamation of Jesus. This ill treatment and hostility was not because of them, but because of "the way and the truth and the life" (John 14:6) of Jesus Christ. The mission of Jesus Christ attracts persecution because the enemy's desire is to stop, hinder, and discourage as many as he can to abandon the life-saving mission of God.

When I became saved, no one warned me about the persecution and attacks of the enemy. In my opinion, many Christians expect to enter into what I call a rose parade. They think that Christianity means life will become rosy now and there will be constant cheering for us. Wrong!

Of course, we don't really want to embrace persecution. That doesn't even sound right. Jesus said that the world will hate us because it hated him first (John 15:18). He promised that since they persecuted him, then naturally, they will persecute us (v. 20). Paul assures us in Acts 14:22 that in order to enter the kingdom of God, "we must go through many hardships." Matthew 13:21 teaches that the persecution that causes some to fall away is because of the Word of God. The enemy of God and of us wants to snuff out the powerful and authoritative Word of the Lord.

After Peter and John prayed for God to move, the place where they were meeting was shaken, they were filled with the Holy Spirit, and they "spoke the word of God boldly" (Acts 4:31). Even in the midst of their persecution, they spoke the Word of God with boldness. This is why the

unleashed

enemy wants to snuff out the Word of the Lord. He wants to take away the Spirit's power!

When we embrace persecution, we embrace the same suffering that allows us to identify more with Christ. He suffered, and so will we because of our association with him. Another reason we embrace persecution is because it compels us to move. The nature of the Spirit of God is just that—he moves. The church is forced to get beyond its comfort zone and rely heavily on the Spirit, the Word, and the will of God. As a result of the heavy persecution brought on the early church, the church spread to other parts of the world. Persecution caused believers not only to depend on God but also to be interdependent on each other—praying together, connecting with one another, and meeting in private, intimate settings to learn the Word and encourage one another.

Stepping Up Our Game

Sometimes an athlete plays to the level of his competition. He may relax when he feels like the opponent is less of a threat to his success. But when he faces a formidable or threatening opponent, his game often rises to a higher level. That threat in competition is like a fire that causes him to respond with the same level of intensity or force that is brought against him.

Without the persecution causing the fire that was lit under them, would the early church have moved as it did? Without persecution or fire under us, will *we* move as we should? Persecution is the antidote for apathy and complacency—the poisons in the church that render us unfit for the kingdom agenda. Persecution keeps us on our toes.

The greater the resistance, the greater the response. The thicker the batter is when a baker is preparing a cake, the greater the strength the baker must use to stir the batter. Likewise, the greater the resistance of the enemy against the church, the more the church must embrace the persecution by faithfully calling on the name of the Lord to fight the battle that is rightfully his.

The Spirit of God Recites the Word of God

In the beginning, God's Word came by the Spirit (see Genesis 1:1-3). Prophecy never came from the will of man, but prophets "were moved by the Holy Spirit, and they spoke from God" (2 Peter 1:21, *NLT*). Where the Word is, so should the Spirit of God be, because God's Word will never come forth without his Spirit. God perpetually reveals himself to us by his original self-expression: his Word.

> "Everything I've learned came from being uncomfortable."

The Word of God transforms. The Word of God heals. The Word of God trains in righteousness (2 Timothy 3:16).

For over a year I've been discipling a young man who has had to deal with a lot of bitterness toward his father. He had little to no respect for his dad because of the things he had witnessed his father do during the young man's growing-up years. After a few weeks of studying the source and effects of pride in the Scriptures, my friend confessed his sin of holding on to an unforgiving attitude toward his father. He began to realize how pride had kept him in that place. Months went by. The more he read the Word of God, the more he realized how that pride had been rearing its head in other areas of his life—including his relationship with his wife. Not too long ago, he commented to me, "Everything I've learned came from being uncomfortable." The Word of God revealed things about himself, and it

unleashed

made him uncomfortable—enough to submit to the Word and allow the Spirit of God to cleanse and sanctify his heart.

We will never boldly transform our communities and, ultimately, the world around us with the Word if we do not first embrace unity in the Spirit. We will not train up a generation to live morally righteous in the eyes of God without introducing them to the Word of God and teaching them to respond to persecution with obedience to the Spirit, rather than cowering under the comfort and convenience of complacency.

Teaching others the Word of God happens within the context of discipleship, using Jesus' model for imparting truth by investing time with others—as he spent time with his twelve disciples. In my short history of part-time lay ministry and full-time vocational ministry, I have had the privilege of watching dozens of men and women that I have helped to mentor be transformed by the powerful Word of God. I have literally seen God begin to shake up a generation with his Word.

They have prayed for and led family members and friends to the Lord.

I lead the Vine, the young adult ministry of Shepherd of the Hills Church. I am careful to teach the Word of God with passion and conviction. Over the course of the last two years, I have watched a group of young adults be transformed—and then evidence that by serving people inside and outside the church. They have started their own ministries to the poor and homeless in the city of Los Angeles, they have prayed for and led family members and friends to the Lord, they have forgiven people who have hurt them grievously. They have done this through mutual encouragement, peer accountability, and with a spirit of unity . . . in ways they previously had not trusted or known before. As I have walked beside them, they've gone through valleys of persecution and trials. But

unleashed

their unity, their oneness, has been a critical component in helping them to overcome. And as a result, they have witnessed God's power moving among their group.

A Whole Lot of Shakin'

God desires to shake up our lives so that through us he can shake up our cities, our schools, our country, and our world for his glory. He wants to do it with the combined force of his Word and his Spirit. What are we willing to embrace in order for us to participate with this move of God? What are we willing to invest as owners of our faith so that the CEO of the entire franchise (Jesus) leaves his mark on the hearts of billions who are lost in darkness?

When God shook the building where the disciples were, he was responding to the prayers of the righteous. They prayed with a spirit of unity. They did not pray in *fear* of the persecution—they prayed in *response* to the persecution. Their prayer is a picture of what it means to embrace unity, the body of Christ pulling together in a time of crisis. They did not choose to flee, fear, or cower under the threat of persecution; they called on the name of the almighty God.

> They did not pray in *fear* of the persecution—they prayed in *response* to the persecution.

In the midst of persecution or trials, we may be inclined to turn and run, to compromise, to fight on our own, or simply to complain about the circumstances. Rather, we must stand and embrace persecution and then fall to our knees in prayer to God in the name of the all-powerful Savior we have in Jesus Christ. Embrace unity and excite the Spirit of God. Embrace persecution and allow it to incite the Spirit of God to cause a great shake-up in your world.

Where do you need to:

unleashed

- welcome unity in your church and ministry?
- embrace unity in your community and home?
- stand on the truth of God's Word in the midst of persecution and trials in your workplace or on your school campus?

The first-century church understood that it took unity among them to excite God. They understood that the threat against the church, although not easy to deal with, could incite God to move. What are you willing to embrace today so that you too can be a vessel whom God will use to shake up a dying world? What are you waiting for?

lavishness

Acts 4:32-37

I have been fortunate enough to have the privilege of working beside and then following Bob Russell as the senior minister at Southeast Christian Church in Louisville, Kentucky. Last November, Bob Russell and Dave Faust, president of Cincinnati Christian University, both wrote to me, requesting that Southeast make a significant gift of $250,000 for the Russell School of Ministry. Part of the reason this scholarship fund was established was to honor Bob's father, who had scraped by in order to send his children to the school, known at the time as the Cincinnati Bible Seminary. The goal was to use the money toward a scholarship fund for students who wanted to preach.

The most the church had ever given to the college was $50,000. The church's eldership discussed the topic, and to my surprise they didn't back down from the number. They embraced the concept of sending a strong message to potential preaching students.

So I sat down with Bob the next week for breakfast, and after some small talk I happily announced, "Hey, the elders decided that we want to give $125,000 to the Russell School of Ministry."

Bob replied, "Wow, thank you so much. I can't believe the church is going to do that much."

I paused and added, "And early next year we are going to give *another* $125,000." I wish you could have seen the look on his face that was somewhere between surprise and joy.

He said, "That's unbelievable. I'm so proud of our church!"

I share that story as a prelude to this chapter. Here's my question for you: Was that gift a *lavish* gift? After all, lavishness isn't an everyday word.

It means extravagant, generous, and abundant. There's no limit to lavishness. That may explain why it can sometimes be misinterpreted as reckless and wasteful. It's something you heap on and pour out in generous measures. That was the largest single gift that our church had ever given to a Bible college, so in that sense it was lavish. But don't simply equate lavishness with giving or generosity.

Lavishness Permeates Everyday Behavior

When you perform an anonymous act of service, buy a meal for a young couple, or send an unexpected check to your adult children, it brings joy to them. Your generosity puts a smile on their faces and causes their hearts to be warmed, because your actions show that you were thinking of them.

If a river is purest at the source, then Christians today should go back to the source—the early Christians in the early church—for the purest example of actions they should strive to imitate. When the church began, those believers left us a blueprint to follow in the area of lavishness. Acts 4 gives us some insights into this characteristic of Christians in the first century. Verses 32-35 say:

All the believers were one in heart and mind. No one claimed that any of their possessions was their own, but they shared everything they had. With great power the apostles continued to testify to the resurrection of the Lord Jesus. And God's grace was so powerfully at work in them all that there were no needy persons among them. For from time to time those who owned land or houses sold them, brought the money from the sales and put it at the apostles' feet, and it was distributed to anyone who had need.

Did you see it? Lavishness permeated their everyday behavior. If someone was in need, the church didn't contact a social agency; instead, they took care of it with the resources that God had entrusted to them. Such expressions of service and love beg that we ask ourselves a tough question: In today's church, are we willing to display such lavishness?

Share Lavishly

Listen to what Paul writes in 2 Corinthians 9:7: "God loves a cheerful giver." Allow me to unpack that phrase a little. The Greek word we translate into English as *cheerful* in that verse is *hilaron,* from which we get the word *hilarious.*[1] I don't want

> I don't want to read too much into the original meaning, but the idea of "hilarious giving" conjures up a great image, doesn't it? It's outrageous!

to read too much into the original meaning, but the idea of "hilarious giving" conjures up a great image, doesn't it? It's outrageous! It provides such incredible pleasure that it doubles you over and brings side-splitting joy and laughter. It's hilarious sharing with a purpose. It's lavish!

Paul is saying, "God loves it when we share liberally and lavishly." It's sharing that the world can't understand, because to them it doesn't make sense. Such sharing truly doesn't make any sense *IF* you believe that *you* own everything. But if you believe God owns everything and entrusts it to your care, then being lavish makes perfect sense . . . especially when you stop and think, *Hmm, who will God bless?* He's going to bless those he knows will do what he wants with the resources he entrusts to them.

Several years ago one of my kids was invited to a birthday party. On the invitation the birthday girl, Kathryn, wrote, "Instead of bringing me a gift, please bring a gift card for a local grocery in any amount, and we'll share it with our local food pantry." It was around Thanksgiving, so

unleashed

Kathryn thought a gift card would be a nice addition to the food basket the food pantry was getting together.

How cool is that, when a twelve-year-old says, "I've got enough stuff!" and she walks away with no gifts? The kids who attended her birthday party brought a total of $360 in gift cards. She brought joy to so many families that Thanksgiving with her creative generosity.

Love Lavishly

If we truly love others lavishly, then we will go *beyond what is expected* to seek out people. We'll reach out to some childhood friends, some over-looked coworkers, some draining neighbors. You might seek out some longtime friends, and maybe some casual acquaintances or strangers whom you want to influence. Paul talks about how we show complete love to others: "Love must be sincere. Hate what is evil; cling to what is good. Be devoted to one another in love. Honor one another above yourselves. . . . Bless those who persecute you; bless and do not curse" (Romans 12:9, 10, 14).

> Sometimes for those of us in ministry, our "love" and concern for others becomes quite predictable and generic.

It could be as simple as sending a card or e-mail to someone and saying that you love him or her. It will take five minutes of your time, but you will never regret it. This act in and of itself is not lavish, but a constant attitude of thinking like this can lead to a lifestyle of lavish love for others. This kind of love involves loving in a way that is unexpected and extraordinary. Sometimes for those of us in ministry, our "love" and concern for others becomes quite predictable and generic. But when someone goes the extra mile to take risks to express lavish love, I take note of it.

Several years ago one of my ministry friends, Jamie Snyder, was serving with a church in Florida. He made a decision to do something rather unique. He felt the Lord leading him to try and talk with an abortion doctor (who happened to be Muslim) in the area where he preached. More specifically, Jamie sensed an urging to simply begin to build a relationship with this man. So he went with another person from his church and brought some gifts and a card to this doctor. They thought they would just be dropping it off with a receptionist, but when she went back and told the doctor, he was intrigued by the gift and told the receptionist that he would take a minute to meet these two. They went back to his office, and the doctor asked, "What is it that you want?"

Jamie said, "We're from a local church, and we just wanted to introduce ourselves and bring a gift by so we could apologize for the way some Christians have treated you."

"But you all *personally* haven't treated me badly," he said, then added, "You do understand that I perform abortions?"

Jamie responded, "Yes, and we couldn't disagree with you more on that. But we're sorry that some Christians haven't always conveyed their disagreement in the best way."

The doctor began to open up and share story after story of attacks, vandalism, and threats made against him by people who opposed abortion. After an hour and repeated requests from the receptionist to tend to his waiting patients, the doctor said, "I've got to get back to my practice," and he thanked them. Jamie then asked if he could pray for him. So he did. Then as Jamie was leaving the office, he said to this doctor, "When it comes to Christians, you probably know what things we are against. But you may not know what we are *for*."

And the abortion doctor said, "You are right. Just what are you *for*?"

Jamie answered, "Here's what we are for: love, joy, peace, patience, kindness, goodness, faithfulness, gentleness, and self-control."

That is the essence of lavish love—doing more than is expected, giving more than is deserved. Maybe that's why Jesus said, "By this

unleashed

everyone will know that you are my disciples, if you love one another" (John 13:35).

Jamie's job was just to love the doctor completely. Lavishly. Not to approve of what he does—what he does is appalling—but to lovingly try to connect this Muslim abortion doctor to Jesus.

Lavish love takes risks. I challenge you to get out of your comfort zone and love someone lavishly. Choose someone who has been overlooked or ignored—perhaps one who is your polar opposite when it comes to spiritual beliefs or political views. It will be a stretch, but high risks can bring high rewards.

> Choose someone who has been overlooked or ignored—perhaps one who is your polar opposite when it comes to spiritual beliefs or political views.

Serve Lavishly

Another way to display lavishness is through serving others. It may be some act of service that is totally unexpected. Perhaps you could serve even a stranger in the most menial of ways.

My church, Southeast Christian, has been blessed to have many generous, loving, lavish givers throughout our history. Last year we asked our folks to buy gifts for the children of single parents and needy families, which would be given out at Christmastime. We received so many toys that Southeast was able to provide five toys per child. Additionally, we were able to give the remaining toys to four other organizations that were in dire need. People volunteered to greet clients, walk alongside clients and help them choose their gifts, wrap gifts, load cars . . . Our volunteers were bold in asking the families if they could pray for them. It was awesome to see small pockets of people praying together each night that this gift-giving took place.

One member of Southeast, a single mom, shopped our Toy Store for her family and then came back the following night, along with her children, and wrapped gifts for others. She wanted her children to understand the importance of giving back. You see, lavish service promotes lavish giving.

Not long before his death, Jesus described how his true followers would be distinguished from those who are not: "Then the righteous will answer him [*that is, King Jesus*], 'Lord, when did we see you hungry and feed you, or thirsty and give you something to drink? When did we see you a stranger and invite you in, or needing clothes and clothe you? When did we see you sick or in prison and go to visit you?' The King will reply, 'Truly I tell you, whatever you did for one of the least of these brothers and sisters of mine, you did for me'" (Matthew 25:37-40).

> Followers of Christ are to be distinctive—to take some risks and express passionate love.

When you are faithful in your service—in the small things and in lavish ways—that Scripture tells us that you are doing it for Jesus. So look around, see the needs, and try to meet them. There are some who legalistically tithe their income and wouldn't miss an opportunity to give to their church. But they struggle to be generous when it comes to service. For too many it's easier to write a check than to pick up a towel and basin and physically serve others. That kind of inconsistency diminishes one's witness and conveys a one-dimensional view of generosity.

Christ is saying to us, "Get out of your comfort zone . . . love completely . . . serve lavishly!" What's the big deal if you just love those who love you? Jesus said, "If you love only those who love you, what reward is there for that? Even corrupt tax collectors do that much" (Matthew 5:46, *NLT).* Followers of Christ are to be distinctive—to take some risks and express passionate love.

unleashed

Give Lavishly

Look back at Acts 4. We find an example of a lavish giver in verses 36, 37: "Joseph, a Levite from Cyprus, whom the apostles called Barnabas (which means 'son of encouragement'), sold a field he owned and brought the money and put it at the apostles' feet." What an encourager he was to the early church. His lavish gift brought joy to God.

Lavishness is part of God's DNA, and you were created in his image. He's a giving God and is able to make all grace abound. He is the giver of every good and perfect gift. You are growing in Christlikeness and in the Father's image when you give. John 3:16 begins, "For God so loved the world that he *gave* . . ." (emphasis added).

We are challenged in Deuteronomy 15:10: "Give generously to [needy brothers] and do so without a grudging heart; then because of this the LORD your God will bless you in all your work and in everything you put your hand to."

John urges us, "Dear children, let us not love with words or speech but with actions and in truth" (1 John 3:18). God wants more than your words of praise, more than your heart and your feelings; he wants you to love him with your gifts and abilities, to love him in a way that can be demonstrated. God wants you to love him lavishly with a love that is seen and demonstrated recklessly on a daily basis.

One of the best biblical examples of how lavishness brings joy to God is found in John 12. Jesus was at a dinner banquet. Martha's sister Mary (not his mother, but one of his followers) was there. After approaching Jesus and pouring a pint of pure nard (an expensive perfume) all over his feet, she proceeded to wipe his feet with her hair. The Bible tells us that the perfume was of incredible value.

Verses 4-6 say: "One of [Jesus'] disciples, Judas Iscariot, who was later to betray him, objected, 'Why wasn't this perfume sold and the money given to the poor? It was worth a year's wages.' He did not say this because he cared about the poor but because he was a thief; as keeper of the money bag, he used to help himself to what was put into it."

The Scriptures are silent concerning how Mary obtained this precious ointment. Perhaps it was a family inheritance or something that she had purchased with her life savings. At any rate, Judas was right on target in saying that this pint of pure nard was worth a year's wages (around 300 denarii). In the Gospel accounts of Matthew and Mark, it says that all the disciples complained about the extravagance—obviously Judas initiated the complaint and cleverly stated his case so that the others would chime in to support him.

Judas was a master of deception. He suggested a commendable alternative to pouring all this money on top of someone's dirty, smelly feet: "Why didn't she give it to the poor?" Of course, Judas's motives were selfishness and greed—from time to time he helped himself to what was in the money bag. We need to be aware that sometimes reservations about lavishness can sound logical.

> Judas knew the perfume and its price tag, but Mary knew it only as a priceless expression of her love for Christ—a lavish gift she would never regret giving.

I should clarify here. When I'm speaking about lavishness, I'm not talking about being wasteful. There is a difference between being frivolous and being generous. Try to understand and catch the big picture; otherwise, like Judas, you'll go through life knowing the cost of everything and the value of nothing. Judas knew the perfume and its price tag, but Mary knew it only as a priceless expression of her love for Christ—a lavish gift she would never regret giving.

I failed to tell you why this banquet had been thrown in Jesus' honor. It was because Lazarus, Mary's brother, had been raised from the dead by Jesus (which is a pretty good reason to party!).

Reasons for Living a Lavish Life

Do you have any reasons to lavishly express generosity and love to God? Has he done anything in your life? Has he:

- forgiven your sin?
- healed your marriage?
- sustained you through an illness?
- reconciled a relationship?
- redeemed your kids?

The list is endless. Genuine, lavish love wants what is best for the other person. Jesus knew this would probably be the last time that Mary would have the opportunity to express her appreciation to him before he was crucified, so he allowed her to perform her act of service.

Lavish Giving Brings Joy to God

I heard a story about Bob McEwen, who served as an Ohio congressman from 1981 to 1992.

Years ago he took his young son to a McDonald's restaurant. McEwen said, "I bought him a Coke and a large order of fries, and we sat in one of those tables that's not built big enough for people to sit in. After a couple of minutes, I reached over to take a french fry. My son put his hands around the fries, blocked them, and pulled them back. I started to reach over again, and my son instinctively put his protective shield up. So I said, 'That's OK.'"

McEwen continued, "As I sat there, I started thinking to myself, *Doesn't my son realize that I'm the one who gave him those fries in the first place? Doesn't he realize I have the strength to take those fries away from him anytime I want? Doesn't he realize I could go up to the counter and that I've got enough money to buy so many fries that I could say, 'Bury my son in french fries? Doesn't my son realize I don't* need *any of his fries; I could go get my* own? All I want to do is share a couple of them with him."

And then the congressman said that it hit him—his son was simply acting like *he* (the congressman) had been acting with God. God blesses us and says, "I want to sit down with you and enjoy some of those blessings." And yet, when he sits down at our table, we selfishly gather our hands around all our stuff and say, "No, no, no. This is ours, God. We'll decide what we're going to give to you."

God in Heaven must say to himself, *Don't they realize I'm the source of everything they've got? I've got the power to take whatever blessings I've given them? Don't they realize I could bury them in blessings (or in struggles) if I wanted to? I don't* need *anything they have—I just wanted to share with them what they've received from my lavish love!*

Your lavishness brings joy to God. Does it blow your mind that whether you are rich or poor, *you* have the ability to put a smile on the face of God?

Lavishness brings joy to others and to God—but lavishness also brings joy to us. God asks us to be generous; and when we are obedient and do it cheerfully, we learn that there is an intrinsic benefit to being generous. Paul said in Acts 20:35, "The Lord Jesus himself said: 'It is more blessed to give than to receive.'" Just as a child is happy that he or she has been obedient, in the same way *we* are happy when we give lavishly.

I believe the level of your joy is in direct proportion to how cheerfully you give. In other words, the more you realize that God owns and we simply manage, the more you believe in the ministry or the cause, the more you are giving out of desire rather than coercion . . . *then* the more joy you'll experience as you give lavishly.

Warren Wiersbe said, "An open heart cannot maintain a closed hand."[2] We give with a willing heart and a happy heart because God loves a cheerful giver. Apparently our attitude—when we give—matters

unleashed

a whole lot to God; maybe it matters even more than how much we give. But if we mutter under our breath every time the offering is taken, or we smolder inside every time we give to a Bible college scholarship fund, then we might be undermining our own blessing from God. Generosity should bring joy. And if we're unable to show generosity to others—and to God—then we have a problem.

Exemplary Lavishness

The apostle Paul held up the Macedonians as an example of lavishness. Second Corinthians 8:2-5 tells us: "In the midst of a very severe trial, their overflowing joy and their extreme poverty welled up in rich generosity. For I testify that they gave as much as they were able, and even beyond their ability. Entirely on their own, they urgently pleaded with us for the privilege of sharing in this service to the Lord's people. And they exceeded our expectations: They gave themselves first of all to the Lord, and then by the will of God also to us."

"Entirely on their own, they urgently pleaded with us for the privilege of sharing in this service to the Lord's people."

Did you notice that they pleaded for the opportunity to give? In essence that's what you may have done when you spoke with your church leaders after the news of a hurricane, earthquake, or flood. At times of crises like these, Christians often beg to get involved in the process. They look for ways to give.

The Macedonians didn't use their lack of funds as an excuse; they translated it into generosity. It is widely believed that the Macedonian church was a poor church. No doubt Satan whispered to them, "Plenty of other churches are better off economically. *They* should be helping. You should look out for number one."

Have you ever known the thrill that comes from being a part of something that is bigger than yourself that requires sacrificial, lavish giving? Paul continued in 2 Corinthians 8:7: "Since you excel in everything—in faith, in speech, in knowledge, in complete earnestness and in the love we have kindled in you—see that you also excel in this grace of giving."

I was fortunate to grow up in a home where my parents modeled lavish giving to the Lord and others in a very natural way. My dad had worked at a Christian college for several years, and then he took a position at a Christian publishing company. So during the early 1980s, because of their knowledge of the pay level of their Bible college cronies, my parents would enlist my brother and me in a series of covert operations.

Periodically, my parents would put $20 or $50 in an envelope and either type or generically write in big block letters the name of a professor. Then it was our job, after the staff had gone home and the cleaning crew had left, to slide an envelope under the person's office door. No one ever knew it was from my parents, and we didn't let anyone know either. But can I tell you something? My parents derived incredible joy from anonymous giving. And so did Jeff and I from just getting to be the delivery boys. Do you think our parents' example motivated us to become stingy or generous?

How can it be that anonymous lavish giving could bring such happiness and fulfillment? I'll tell you why: because Jesus assures us there is someone who knows of our secret unselfishness. In Matthew 6:3, 4, Jesus said, "When you give to the needy, do not let your left hand know what your right hand is doing, so that your giving may be in secret. Then your Father, who sees what is done in secret, will reward you."

There is within each one of us a carnal desire to hoard and keep. It's a temptation for me to stay in acquisition mode rather than relinquishing

unleashed

what I've accumulated. But that's the opposite of lavishness. One of the most freeing things you can do is to hold on to the things of this world loosely. That allows you to give lavishly.

Twenty-five years ago my godly grandmother passed away. A couple of years after that, my grandfather decided that he would sell the farm equipment and my grandmother's belongings at a public auction to provide cash for things *he* wanted. He was in a pattern of making unwise choices, and he would not be dissuaded.

> One of the most freeing things you can do is to hold on to the things of this world loosely. That allows you to give lavishly.

As you can imagine, the day of the auction was very emotional. Furniture, farm implements, and household goods were displayed. I later learned that the children were given no chance to purchase even items of sentimental value ahead of time.

One of the family keepsakes my mother was interested in was a beautiful, wedding-ring design, handmade quilt. Since my grandmother had loved that quilt, my mom really wanted to have it. However, a determined antique dealer wanted to purchase it and then resell it.

Through the course of time, the bidding reached a point beyond my mom's self-imposed spending limit. It was more than she could bear, so she turned and left the bidding area while the auctioneer continued to watch the bids go higher. But moments later a strange scene unfolded as my older brother, Jeff, who was a dirt-poor preacher in his mid-twenties and who had absolutely no earthly interest in quilts, began bidding. Several minutes later the auctioneer announced, "Sold!" and they folded up Jeff's purchase. He walked out of the auction barn, found Mom, handed her the quilt, and said, "I love you." They hugged and we cried.

Years later my brother would say, "I spent more than I really had. I paid more than I probably should have. But I have never regretted buying that quilt."

That's a powerful example of lavish giving, freely sharing and thinking of others above self. When we give like that, God promises to bless our generosity. He always brings things full circle according to his perfect will and timing.

What If the Church Gave Lavishly?

The church today would be unleashed if we all gave generously.

- How many more churches could we start?
- How many more missionaries could we support?
- How many more souls could we rescue?
- How many more young people could we send to Bible college?

What would happen if everyone in the church today sacrificially gave with abandon? I challenge your church to take on a project so big, it will only succeed if God is in it. I challenge *you* personally to do the same.

> I challenge your church to take on a project so big, it will only succeed if God is in it.

I began by telling you about a breakfast meeting with Bob Russell when I shared the news about our church committing $250,000 to Cincinnati Christian University. That day as we were wrapping up our breakfast time, I asked if Bob would be interested in team teaching with me in a series on stewardship in a couple of months. I suggested that we could talk about how prudent Bob had been with the church's finances through the years and how he had learned generosity and sacrifice from his father.

We each began to brainstorm some of the topics and illustrations that we could work into that message. I mentioned a story Bob used to tell about when he was young. The preacher at their home church had skipped town and stuck the church and creditors with thousands of dollars of bills. Understand that this took place in the early 1960s. In order to protect the reputation of the church in the community, Bob's father took out a loan to pay off the preacher's debts, and then he took a second job in order to pay off the loan.

Upon being reminded of that story, Bob asked me, "Do you know how much my dad borrowed to pay off those debts? It was $2,500." Then he paused and said, "Do you know what's a hundred times $2,500?"

I thought for a second, looked up from my plate, and answered, "$250,000." When I saw that Bob's eyes were filled with tears, the significance of the number hit me. For some time that morning two grown men sat there, with lumps in their throats, unable to speak.

Finally, Bob broke the silence and quoted Christ's words, "Everyone who has left houses or brothers or sisters or father or mother or wife or children or fields for my sake will receive a *hundred* times as much and will inherit eternal life" (Matthew 19:29, emphasis added).

God had allowed the lavish generosity and service of a humble servant, nearly half a century before, to multiply exponentially in order to encourage the school where all six of his children had attended. Still today, each of those children serves in some type of Christian ministry. Charles Russell must have chuckled from above, had he overheard our breakfast conversation.

The joy of lavish giving cannot be fully understood or accepted until it has been experienced. You don't listen to a sermon or read a chapter in a book and become convinced. You have to take a step of faith and express your love, service, and generosity in lavish proportions. I guarantee that you won't regret it now, nor will you in fifty years.

hazardous

Acts 5:17-42

Once a year, for the past three years, I have made the long journey from Los Angeles to Rwanda to preach in prisons that house Hutus responsible for a carefully orchestrated genocide that systematically slaughtered eight hundred thousand people. I first went because God opened the door; I continue to go because prisoners keep responding to the message of the gospel, repenting before God and reconciling with the families from which they took precious lives. Each year I complain about the long flights and cramped spaces, the stale food and hard beds, the rough roads and outrageous price of gas. I complain because I'm used to convenience, comfort, and lower prices in affluent America.

On my most recent trip, after spending three weeks in Africa, seeing firsthand the sacrifices African pastors make to proclaim the gospel, I realized what a weak-minded, weak-willed, pathetic person I really am. Anastase, my translator, transported me into the mountains near the Congo border to preach in one of Rwanda's more restricted prisons. Evidently, he wanted to up the ante! This particular prison houses the elite—the government officials and district leaders who may never have swung a machete but are no less responsible for crimes against humanity.

After three hours of intensive driving that featured constant warnings from Anastase to remain close to his side while inside the prison, I looked him in the eye and asked, "Anastase, are we in any danger?"

Without missing a beat, he stared straight back at me and emphatically questioned, "Does it matter?"

Wow! Three small words revealed the truth about me: I am interested in doing God's work as long as it isn't hazardous. I can picture Jesus' recruiting agents stamping "REJECTED" on my application for discipleship.

New Life

"You will probably be arrested, thrown in prison, abandoned, or disowned by your own families—and ultimately lose your earthly inheritance."

By modern-day standards, Jesus was a horrible recruiter. Imagine being interviewed and told, "OK guys, if you want to be on my team, be aware that you will be running for your lives most of the time. In fact, you will be like sheep being pursued by wolves. You will be flogged. [*Mel Gibson's vivid scourging scene in* The Passion of the Christ *comes to mind.*] You will probably be arrested, thrown in prison, abandoned, or disowned by your own families—and ultimately lose your earthly inheritance. So are you in?" (my loose paraphrase of Matthew 10:11-23).

Most of us would be running for the door. But then, on your way out, you are also told that you will be given the power of new life! This new life is the Spirit of the living God who will enable you to do things you have never done, see things you have never seen, and feel things you have never felt. Moreover, this new life brings a new power that, when unleashed, changes the world!

OK, so maybe I'm in, after all!

Elation replaces concern . . . until you hear the caution repeated: "But it *is* true that the road on which you are asked to travel will be fraught with peril!"

In short, the way of the Christ follower is hazardous, and yet this is the story of the first church. Despite constant threats of severe beatings and other daily hazards, they continued to proclaim the good news of Jesus Christ (see Acts 5:17-42).

Clear and Present Danger

History often speaks of Rome's persecution against the church, but here in the book of Acts, Rome was not the perpetrator. Acts 5 is perhaps the first account of a competing religion (Judaism) attempting to crush Christianity, not out of passion for truth but out of jealousy (large crowds were following the disciples; see v. 16) and fear (many of these followers believed that the Messiah had come and that these religious leaders were responsible for his death; see v. 28).

Make no mistake, the first church faced a clear and present danger, but they were not about to back down. They had followed a rabbi who taught them that obeying God was much more important than fearing man—so they pressed on (v. 29).

Peter and the other apostles understood the importance of evangelism and an essential ingredient to its success: one's passion for proclaiming Christ must exceed one's passion for self-preservation. A person must pick up his cross daily and follow Jesus (Luke 9:23). He must embrace the truth that the power of God will be unleashed through him in direct proportion to the degree that he is willing to die to himself.

For us today, especially in America where physical persecution seems unlikely, I believe the type of hazardous living to which we are called falls into three categories: hazardous faith, hazardous grace, and hazardous sacrifice.

> The first church faced a clear and present danger, but they were not about to back down.

Yes, I am aware of the warnings that Christians will be the Jews of the twenty-first century. I am aware that our stance on issues such as abortion, same-sex marriage, and other moral hotbeds may bring the God-haters out of the woodwork, firing verbal darts and philosophical bullets at the Christian community. But that is simply not the same

unleashed

thing as the physical persecution our brothers faced in the early church. Neither is it similar to what many Christ followers experience every day in Sudan, northern India, Indonesia, and China. Nevertheless, the hazards we face are just as real and, if not faced with great courage, will stifle the expansion of Christ's kingdom in the world.

Hazardous Faith

I was twenty-three years old and living in Zimbabwe, Africa, a rookie to ministry and a novice in my faith. I guess God decided he needed me to grow up fast, so he sent a giant. Like David facing Goliath, I was forced to decide whether I really trusted God to provide the victory or whether I would cower away in fear and discouragement. Looking back now, I think courage chose me.

Eight o'clock Saturday morning there was a violent knock at the door. Patrick, barely a teenager, stood in the doorway.

"Pastor Jeff, come quickly! Verice is in the hospital! He was injured playing rugby and lies in a coma. The doctors say he is not going to make it."

Verice's father, Mr. Mashonga, was the chief of the village and held the respect of the entire community. "If you want the villagers, go after the village leader" was a lesson I had learned rather quickly. So for one solid month, we had prayed that God would move in Mr. Mashonga's life, that God would orchestrate and fashion together events that would open Mr. Mashonga's eyes to the truth of the gospel. And now, just as the thirty days were complete, his treasured son lay lifeless in a hospital bed. All the way to the hospital, I kept filing my complaint with God: "Why have you allowed this? Why didn't you prevent such a tragedy?"

All the way to the hospital, I kept filing my complaint with God: "Why have you allowed this?"

unleashed

126

Passing the waiting area adjacent to the emergency room, I paused, greatly moved in spirit by the sorrow of Verice's family. The Shona culture holds nothing back when it comes to expressing grief, and this scene was no exception. Mr. Mashonga, grasping the seriousness of Verice's condition, issued a challenge, variations of which I had heard many times before: "If your God is as powerful and loving as you claim he is, then ask him to make my son well."

Swept suddenly by waves of fear, panic, and pressure, I could feel things spiraling out of control. I had no answer for this. Furthermore, I believed that the request was a fair one. Then again, I thought, *Maybe this has been God's plan from the beginning. Maybe this is how God is going to answer my prayer. I am going to go into that emergency room and raise Verice to life. Yeah God! Outstanding plan! You da man! I mean . . . you da God!* (Sorry.) With a new lease on life, I knelt by Verice's hospital bed and prayed the deepest, most powerful prayer I knew.

> *Maybe this is how God is going to answer my prayer. I am going to go into that emergency room and raise Verice to life.*

"God, please heal my friend. This is your big chance! Don't miss it, God! If you heal Verice, especially while I am in the room, then they are going to know that my God is a God of power and love! I've got it now, God! Let's roll!"

I sat beside Verice's hospital bed for more than three hours, praying the same prayer over and over again: "God, heal Verice! Bring Verice back to life so the chief might bow to his maker." I kept thinking, *How is this not a good plan? Come on, God, release your divine energy!*

Around six in the evening, Verice died. The nurse requested that I tell the family, so I walked down the hall toward the waiting area, wondering how I would break the news. But as soon as they caught a glimpse of

unleashed

my dejected demeanor, the family began to weep loudly and demonstratively. Aunts, uncles, cousins, and grandparents—devastated at the loss of a child so well loved—held nothing back in their shameless display of emotion. Mr. Mashonga, however, stood with a glaring disapproval of both my God and me.

While driving home I began a rather aggressive dialogue with God: "How could you, God? You blew it! This was your big chance! How could you just sit on your hands and do nothing?"

To make matters worse, our Sunday morning service was just hours away. In light of all that had happened, what could I possibly say that would make any difference? Nine-thirty arrived, and I began my walk from the farmhouse to the church building. Turning the corner and moving toward the front entrance, I witnessed a miracle of Red Sea proportions—church members and guests arriving early!

> When the chief asks to have a word with his people, you comply. I stepped aside.

Immediately, I knew I was in over my head. These people were coming for answers, and I had none. My own issues with God remained unresolved, so how could I possibly address theirs? Nevertheless, the praise team launched into worship, and I began counting down the minutes till my sermon. I took my place behind the podium and began to deliver the message I had prepared days before Verice's death—a message that totally ignored the elephant in the room.

Ten minutes into my irrelevant dissertation, Mr. Mashonga, who had never darkened the doors of the church, entered through the back and continued walking until he reached the stage, front and center. Interrupting my sermon, he whispered, "Pastor Jeff, I wonder if I could have a word with my people?"

Well, when the chief asks to have a word with his people, you comply. I stepped aside, sat down with my head in my hands, and wondered how long it would take me to pack my bags and leave town. My ministry was over and I knew it. There was no way God could recover from this. And then Mr. Mashonga leaned forward into the microphone and, with both hands placed on the podium, uttered the following words: "People of the Greencroft Christian Church, as you know, my son Verice passed away yesterday evening. He was my precious son." As tears began to flow, he continued, "This pastor says that his God is powerful and loving. Well, I am not certain of all this, but one thing I do know: ever since my son Verice started coming to this place, he was a better son, a better student, a better man. So I was wondering, whatever it is you gave to him, would you give that to me too?"

And there was silence in Heaven for half an hour—at least that's what it felt like. But then the overjoyed crowd belted into a round of applause that would have raised the roof off most American church buildings. That church would never be the same again—the power of God had been unleashed!

Mr. Mashonga soon discovered that the "thing" Verice had found was Jesus. And like his son, the father bent his knee before Christ and the transformation began. The chief had been saved! Many others soon followed as the receptivity to the gospel catapulted beyond what we could ever hope or imagine. God and I engaged in dialogue of a different kind. This time, he spoke and I listened. I heard no audible voice, but the message was clear: "True faith is trusting in the promises, plan, and providence of God even when things seem out of control, or even downright hazardous!"

Divine Calling

With the crucifixion of Jesus in their recent memory, the disciples understood the reality that one could be in the most hazardous situation conceivable and still be in the very center of God's will. This is precisely

unleashed

why they were able to face the threat of persecution with such courage. So at the risk of receiving more punishment from the high priest and his associates, Peter and the other apostles acted on faith and obeyed God rather than men (Acts 5:29). After the apostles spoke the truth concerning how the teachers of the law had killed Jesus by "hanging him on a cross" (v. 30), the Sanhedrin were furious and ready to put the apostles to death. But a Pharisee named Gamaliel put the brakes on, cautioning them that they'd only find themselves "fighting against God" (v. 39).

His speech persuaded them, and the apostles were beaten and warned again not to speak anymore in the name of Jesus.

> Things may look out of control, events may make little to no sense, but the truth is that God sometimes places us in situations that are terrifying.

If we are to be used of God in dramatic ways, we have to be willing to enter seasons of our lives when God seems silent, trusting that he is fully present and bringing his plan to fruition. That's hazardous faith! Things may look out of control, events may make little to no sense, but the truth is that God sometimes places us in situations that are terrifying, dangerous, even hazardous—and he is trusting that we won't bail.

If you're anything like me in our affluent world, when you don't get what you think you deserve, or when God does not deliver you in the manner you think he should, you often begin to doubt and ask, "Can I trust God?"

I have come to believe that perhaps in difficult times God is asking, "Can I trust *you*? Will you place my purposes at the very top of your priority list so that your personal convenience takes a backseat to what I want to do in the world?" When God knows he can trust us to embrace difficult, hazardous situations with this kind of attitude, he will do immeasurably more than we could ever ask or imagine.

What set of unfortunate circumstances has God allowed in your life or your church as a test of your allegiance and usability? Are you ducking and running for cover? Or are you saying, "OK God, how are you going to use this tragedy to change me? to change the world?" Hazardous faith is the final frontier. It's the willingness to hand everything over to God to do as he sees fit.

At a time when all seemed lost, David gave up trying to manipulate God, sent the ark of the covenant back to Jerusalem, and proclaimed, "Let [God] do to me whatever seems good to him" (2 Samuel 15:26). When we exhibit this type of faith, hazardous times may come, but we can rest assured that God is about to unleash his power, release his divine energy, and change the world!

Mr. Mashonga not only submitted to the lordship of Christ, but later became the chairman of the board of elders and a prominent leader in the Christian church throughout Zimbabwe. But this is not where the story ends.

A sweet little girl named Shingi could often be found on our front porch, coloring an outline of baby Jesus in the manger, sipping orange juice out of a plastic cup, or listening to the Bible stories my wife, Robin, read to her. Talented, beautiful, and full of fire and passion, Shingi grew up to marry Denford Chizanga, the man who would eventually take my place as senior pastor. Under pastor Chizanga's leadership the church would go places it had never been before. In fact, twenty years later Denford and Shingi Chizanga are still setting southern Africa on fire with the gospel and taking territory no missionary has ever taken before. I believe Shingi, one of the strongest and most devoted young women I have ever met, got her passion and

> Hazardous faith is the final frontier. It's the willingness to hand everything over to God to do as he sees fit.

thirst for evangelism not from me or my wife, but from her father . . . the chief, Mr. Mashonga.

Hazardous Grace

Tempted to preach only the dos and don'ts of their new faith, the early church had to be reminded that the essential, fundamental aspect of Jesus' teaching emphasized grace (see Galatians 5). But grace, as beautiful and wonderful as it is, can be hazardous. Some of the most dangerous and unattractive places in our cities, some of the most repulsive and questionable people in our neighborhoods are also the places and people most open and most in need of the good news of God's mercy. Following perhaps the most recognizable verse in the Bible, John 3:16, are found words we often forget: "God did not send his Son into the world to condemn the world, but to save the world through him" (v. 17).

We were going to be face-to-face with men and women who had taken machetes in their hands and mercilessly slaughtered their neighbors and their neighbors' children.

Captivating Encounter

My first experience preaching in the Rwandan prisons came in 2007 with my good friend Mark Hall. Anastase (our translator) escorted our team to a prison just minutes outside the capital city of Kigali. The tension we felt walking through the iron gates clearly communicated that all was not well in the camp. It was twelve years after the genocide, and yet thousands still refused to repent of their atrocities. The three men with whom I traveled did not recognize the magnitude of the situation nor the real and present risk we were taking. (Ignorance is indeed bliss.) However, we knew with great certainty that we were going to be face-to-face with men and women who had taken machetes in their hands and mercilessly slaughtered their neighbors and their neighbors' children. We had toured the genocide memorial just days earlier, and images of the horror of machetes coming down on the heads and necks of young children were still fresh in our minds. Now God was reaching out, offering grace and forgiveness to people who had refused to grant it to others.

Knowing the task was truly impossible—outside of a dramatic move of the Spirit and a forceful taking of enemy territory—a team of chaplains gathered behind me to pray and hope. As soon as I stood up to speak, I knew the Spirit of God was about to take over. Suddenly feeling that what I had prepared was not appropriate, I reached out to God for his favor. (Yes, I know the Spirit of God works just as effectively in preparation as in delivery. But sometimes, rare as those times may be, God intervenes and strongly impresses on the speaker to go in a certain direction. This kind of thing happens often near the end of a message when a time for decision comes, but seldom have I experienced it so early in the message.)

After sharing the simple message of the cross, suddenly God's Spirit brought to my mind a children's story written by one of my favorite Christian authors, Ravi Zacharias.[1] My immediate response was, *What? A children's story to thousands of murderers? I don't think so.* But God assured me this was the way to go.

The Broken Promise is a simple story about a brother and sister who trade what is most precious to them. The sister gives up her jar of beautiful, colorful candy in exchange for her brother's prized and precious marbles. Although the arrangement included a full and complete trade, in an act of betrayal the little brother removed some of the more favored stones prior to the exchange. Then, shaking the jar to create the illusion of fullness, he completed the treacherous transaction with his sister. As I approached this part of the story, I was stunned to see the response by the crowd: they booed, hissed, and shouted in protest as if the little boy had committed the unpardonable sin. Think of it! These men and women had slaughtered little children—thousands of them. How could they possibly express vile disapproval of a little boy who stole a few marbles from his sister? But isn't this representative of the human race? It is easy to see sin in the lives of others; it is almost impossible to see it in our own.

Visibly upset by the young boy's act of treason, these prisoners were primed and ready to hear the message of the gospel. Then the Spirit entrusted me with the perfect punch line to the story, "If you give God all your sin, I promise you, he will give you all his forgiveness." I just kept repeating that line over and over. "If you give God all your sin, he will give you all his forgiveness."

Captivating Freedom

Suddenly, sin exposed, eyes opened, hearts softened, and then . . . hope found. I watched with amazement as the Spirit opened eyes to the power of sin and, more importantly, to the reality of forgiveness and grace found in Jesus Christ. People from every direction began making their way down to receive Christ. Tears began to flow, and the Spirit of God seemed to hover over the camp. Our entire team quickly realized that something very special was happening. Mercy had come where none had been given. Grace had fallen on those we least expected.

> Our entire team quickly realized that something very special was happening. Mercy had come where none had been given. Grace had fallen on those we least expected.

As the iron gates closed behind us, we took a deep breath and realized that for an hour or so, we had really lived! Earlier that morning we had no idea what to expect. Uneasy about going into such strange territory, we wondered whether we could actually communicate effectively to people with whom we had very little in common. Moreover, we wondered, would we be in harm's way? Worse yet, some part of us wondered if these machete-wielding murderers even deserved forgiveness. (Yes, I know that's why it's called grace.) The whole experience was risky, uncomfortable, unattractive . . . and hazardous!

Jesus constantly frustrated the religious elite with his refusal to separate himself from sinners. In fact, the argument could be made that Jesus relentlessly pursued those far from God. And after Jesus' ascension into Heaven, the gospel

> I believe it was largely due to the willingness of the church to proclaim grace loudest where it was needed most.

spread like California wildfires and penetrated the hearts of prostitutes, tax collectors, and thieves, as well as lawyers, doctors, and kings. Why? I believe it was largely due to the willingness of the church to proclaim grace loudest where it was needed most.

Can I ask you a personal question? Is this indicative of your evangelistic endeavors? of the endeavors of your church?

Captivating Mercy

After spending twenty years on the mission field and returning home to pastor a megachurch in California, I am somewhat disheartened. Why do we in the contemporary church in America refuse to pursue and, at times, even appear to separate? Yes, there are exceptions. Jim Cymbala, senior pastor of the Brooklyn Tabernacle (a church that has reached out and welcomed drug addicts, transvestites, alcoholics, gays, lesbians, and prostitutes), told me that still today many within the church world criticize his reaching out to so-called reprobates of society.

"I don't want my daughter around those types of people!" religious people say. "What if they come into church with the smell of liquor on their breath?" Or "What if a transvestite shows up at our church and my sixteen-year-old son sees this? What will I say to him?"

I have an easy answer to all the above questions. Jesus said, "It is not the healthy who need a doctor, but the sick" (Matthew 9:12). Jesus called people to repentance, as should we; but he also visited and ate with sinners, and we should not forget to do this as well. When the church begins to engage in hazardous grace, then, and only then, will the church on earth begin to look like the church in Heaven.[2]

Captivating Grace

When Proposition 8 (a proposition forcing voters to accept or reject same-sex marriage) hit the newsstands, homes, and churches of California, every pastor had to make a decision concerning how he and his church would respond. Neutrality was not an option. Neutrality signaled opposition to both sides of the camp. It was the ultimate "either you are for us or against us" scenario. This put the church in a precarious position. The challenge is this: How do we stand for biblical authority without compromising our ability to love, minister to, and embrace those who struggle with the sin of homosexuality?

Wanting to leave nothing to chance, I invited anyone in the church struggling with this sin to a one-on-one meeting to help me better understand the issues. Within hours, I received four e-mails from regular attenders who wanted to talk. One particular e-mail came from a lesbian couple who seemed desperate. I set up an appointment, and we met for a few hours over lunch.

We opened our Bibles and studied God's Word together. Their arguments, given with great respect for the Bible and me, were based more on emotion and pragmatism than objective truth. Their logic went something like this: "How could this be wrong when it feels so right? I did not choose to be like this. God made me like this." I assured them that God had a much better plan and that he did not give his law arbitrarily. If God says there is a line we should not cross, it's because he knows that when such lines *are* crossed, sadness, not joy; death, not life; and depression, not hope, follow.

This desperately needs to be communicated to the current generation. God never intended to be the big, bad, cosmic boss! His laws are motivated by his love. He is our heavenly Father and knows that if we live within the parameters he establishes, the abundant life will be ours. But if we step outside those boundaries, death and destruction lie in wait.

When our conversation was over, the couple asked an interesting question: "Would we be welcomed in your church as we are trying to sort all this out?" In other words, they were asking whether "sinners" were allowed to come to church. I

> God never intended to be the big, bad, cosmic boss! His laws are motivated by his love.

assured them that they would fit right in with everyone else. Yes, I will call them to repentance just like I call everyone else, including myself—but I will also love them on their journey. Would your church do the same?

Until the church unleashes this type of hazardous grace (I am certain there will be church members who would stay as far away as possible from my lesbian friends), it will spend its time debating the style of music, the dress code of the youth pastor, the senior pastor's haircut, and other trivial matters that have no eternal significance!

Want to see a revival in your church? My friend, Cam Huxford, pastor of Savannah Christian Church, likes to say that there is nothing happening in your church that can't be solved with about forty baptisms. When people start getting saved, when we see the transformation of people steeped in sin, when two lesbians discover that all they are looking for

unleashed

can be found in Christ, our attention shifts from our disagreements and problems to worship and praise for the manner in which God is moving in our church. Grace is indeed hazardous, but it will make you feel alive again!

Can I ask: Are your church services a holy huddle? Is everyone saved and the riffraff kept out? You say, "No, Jeff, everyone's welcome." Really? If everyone's welcome, why aren't they coming? Do you take great satisfaction in the affluence of your congregation and your church budget or in the far-reaching effects of grace and love among your people? When hazardous grace is unleashed, people get saved. When people get saved, the church goes from strength to strength, and everyone feels alive!

Hazardous Sacrifice

> Such persecution in no way deterred their fervor for the Great Commission but, instead, was a catalyst for an even greater passion.

The end of Acts 5 highlights the compelling attitude with which the early church faced the hazards associated with following Christ. While we often come to Christ seeking how he may improve the quality of our lives, the first disciples came to him ready to put their lives on the line, if that's what was required to advance Jesus' kingdom. In fact, after suffering a ferocious beating, the disciples, rather than cowering away from their calling, were "rejoicing because they had been counted worthy of suffering disgrace for the Name" (Acts 5:41). Moreover, such persecution in no way deterred their fervor for the Great Commission but, instead, was a catalyst for an even greater passion as they "never stopped teaching and proclaiming the good news that Jesus is the Messiah" (v. 42).

Despite continuous threats and severe floggings, the first-century church carried out Jesus' message of hope that the world would be changed and Christ would reign supreme in the hearts and minds of a new generation. Many counted it a privilege to glorify God not only with their lives but also with their deaths. In John 21:18 Jesus informed Peter that he would be given the supreme opportunity to lay down his life for an eternal cause. We know from oral tradition that when the moment of truth came, Peter lived as though the cause of Christ superseded personal convenience, and he died a martyr's death.

Costly Ordeal

Today in many parts of the world, Christians live under this same constant threat of persecution. Christians in China, for instance, are willing to preach regardless of the cost. In fact, more Christians are in prison in China than any other place in the world.[3] In India, Hindu extremists are presently committing genocide against the Christians in the northern regions. In late August of 2008, Hindu militants committed the worst violations against Christians since independence. Seventy thousand people lost their homes, and fifty thousand now live in refugee camps, fearing the return of the extremists.[4] Then there is the Sudan. Thirty years of persecution have not prevented or stunted the growth of the Sudanese Christian churches.[5]

> Then there is the Sudan. Thirty years of persecution have not prevented or stunted the growth of the Sudanese Christian churches.

In each of those cases, the church, to a significant degree, has been forced underground. Yet it thrives and contains very few lukewarm members. No sacrifice is too great if the result is the expansion of Christ's kingdom on the earth. In fact, many Christians in captive nations no longer build houses for themselves. Such houses become distractions. Dwelling places require money, time, and energy that could be spent on eternal things. If this type of hazardous living were ever to become a present

unleashed

reality in the West, the world would be reached with the gospel, the work of evangelism would be completed, and Christ would return.

Ridiculous? Nonsensical? Unrealistic?

Consider for a moment that 10 percent of the world possesses 85 percent of its wealth.[6] The average American spends 37 percent on housing, 5 percent on apparel, 19 percent on transportation, 4 percent on health care, 5 percent on entertainment, and 13 percent on food. Yet the average Christian gives only 1.5–2.5 percent.[7] That's a far cry from the 10 percent commanded in the Bible.

Richard Stearns, the president of World Vision, said, "If every Christian in America tithed, it would be $168 billion."[8] Twenty-two thousand children die every day from preventable causes.[9] For $30 billion per year, world hunger could be eradicated.[10] For $10 billion more, all the world's children could have clean water,[11] and for just $12 billion more per annum, every child in the world could receive an education.[12]

Imagine what kind of doors would open for the gospel if the Christians in America educated every child, provided clean drinking water for every family, and wiped out hunger. And by the way, that's what the church could do for a meager $52 billion. We would still have $116 billion left over!

Rich Toward God

So what's the problem? We would rather spend it on ourselves! You and I would rather have the latest gadgets than live in obedience toward God. Some will take offense at such a statement and then embark on a journey to defend why tithing is unique to Old Testament law. But the firstfruits principle originated long before the law of Moses. Hundreds of years before Moses, Abraham brought tithes to Melchizedek. Cain, instructed to bring to God the very best of what he had (firstfruits) as an acknowledgment of God's provision, violated the principle and received an unfavorable look for his weak efforts (Genesis 4:2-5). In the New Testament, Jesus reminded those who would listen that giving is a matter of the heart. He categorically stated, "Where your treasure is, there your heart will be also" (Matthew 6:21). We simply cannot escape the truth that what you value most will be clearly visible to the world around you. I wonder what any person from a developing nation would see as our treasure.

But the Spirit of God inspired Paul to make the strongest statement about our attitude concerning money, in 1 Timothy 6:17, 18: "Command those who are rich in this present world not to be arrogant nor to put their hope in wealth, which is so uncertain, but to put their hope in God, who richly provides us with everything for our enjoyment. Command them to do good, to be rich in good deeds, and to be generous and willing to share."

Who are the "rich" of verse 17? We are! Remember, 10 percent of the world possesses 85 percent of its wealth. What is the temptation for those who are affluent? To put our trust in wealth instead of in God. To depend on stuff rather than on God for our happiness. To hoard—living as if the more money we have, the happier we will be. Paul says not to do that! God is the source of your happiness, not money. Instead of being rich in things, the challenge is for us to be rich in good deeds. Jesus called this being "rich toward God" (Luke 12:21).

Sacrilege

Unfortunately, in America *we* (yes, I am equally guilty) tend to live a life of sacrilege. G. Campbell Morgan warned us that *sacrilege* means not only to take something that is sacred and use it in a profane fashion but also can be to "take something and give it to God when it means absolutely nothing to us."[13] In other words, God gets our leftovers, not our very best. He gets our leftover money, our leftover time, and our leftover talents after we have spent the best on ourselves.

If Christians took seriously the command to be rich toward God, then the power of the church would be unleashed upon the world, and the eradication of so much pain and suffering would open the door for the transformation of many souls.

Modern-Day Samaritan

Tony Campolo tells the story of Elias Santana. Born in the Dominican Republic, Santana attended medical school in the United States, where he discovered a personal relationship with Jesus Christ.[14] He returned home to use his gifts, not to become rich but to become rich toward God. Elias Santana would take the one-hour flight to Puerto Rico, make a pile of money performing surgery at the city hospital, then return to the Dominican Republic to work among the poorest of the poor. Using the money he had made in Puerto Rico to buy medical supplies, he would drive into the slums, open up the back of his truck, and begin treating the sick.

After hours and hours of work, he would honk his horn, stand on the top of the truck, and begin preaching the gospel.

On one occasion a prime mover for the Marxist movement happened upon this familiar scene in the ghetto where Santana was preaching Christ. Tony Campolo yelled at the young Marxist, "Hey, Pedro! Elias has the ear of the people. You'd better watch out! He's going to win them all to Christ, and there will be none of them left to follow you."

Without cracking a smile, the young man responded, "What am I supposed to say? Elias Santana has earned the right to be heard."

What We Truly Need

As mentioned previously, for the past three years I have made the journey to Rwanda to preach in the prisons. In the summer of 2010, I agreed to remain in the country for a few extra days to teach and encourage some of Rwanda's most passionate and gifted pastors. Within the first twenty-four hours, it dawned on me that I was the one in need of sermons and encouragement. These pastors live hand to mouth, work extremely long hours, and consider it the highest privilege to suffer for Christ. Each pastor would willingly give his life if it meant the kingdom of God would be expanded.

When the conference was over, I asked Anastase why these men were so committed. His answer? Once again, astounding. Feeling at ease and comfortable in the integrity of our relationship, he said, "Pastor Jeff, this is not rare; this is the way it is

> These pastors live hand to mouth, work extremely long hours, and consider it the highest privilege to suffer for Christ.

supposed to be. The problem with you Americans is that you are distracted by your affluence. Rather than praising God for your blessings, the blessings have become your god and you worship them." Then he placed his arm around me and said, "But Pastor Jeff, change begins with you."

The church has everything it needs to unleash its power on the world. We are not waiting for God. God is waiting for us . . . to engage in hazardous faith, hazardous grace, and hazardous sacrifice. When we choose to do these things, we will become rich toward God and the world will never be the same.

unleashed

kinetic

Acts 13:41-52

L ast fall I was on a flight from my home in Southern California to Seattle. A woman was sitting in my row with an empty seat between us. Something inside told me that I was supposed to talk to her about God. I asked God for an opportunity but basically chickened out and didn't make the effort. I then went to the pastors' gathering, where I preached on . . . courage. Of all things. The whole time I was struck by my failure that morning on the plane.

After speaking I returned to the airport to fly home. When I arrived at my seat, guess who was seated *right next to me?* Do you know how impossible that is? For her to be on the same flight was already amazing, but for her to be seated right next to me was nearly impossible! Even *she* had to know that it couldn't have been a coincidence. I was able to then share with her why I believed God placed her next to me. She opened up about her life, and we had a great conversation. The greatest part is that she had to know God himself was pursuing her. And it was another reminder that God is constantly working with me.

I was in a taxi a few months ago. After discovering that my driver was Muslim, I began asking him questions about his theology. We had a very interesting and friendly talk. I asked him if God answered his prayers. He immediately answered yes. Then I began sharing some of the specific answers to prayers in my life. About five minutes later he confessed, "You know how you asked me whether God answers my prayers? He doesn't. I feel better after praying, but I don't experience the answers." I loved his honesty, which led to a pretty powerful conversation.

Those two experiences were incredible reminders of how God wants to use me for his glory every day. But there are days when I tell the Lord honestly, "I don't feel like serving you right now"—and I don't like that. I'm as lazy and comfort-driven as the next guy. Like almost everyone else I know, I also battle self-centered desires. But I know that every time I do go out and try to make disciples, I'm always grateful afterwards. Then I say to myself, *I can't believe I would have traded that for just another average day.*

Comfort-Driven or Eternity-Driven?

We live in a very comfortable and fun culture, and everything, it seems, is about pleasure. It's hard not to get caught up in that. But when you live in a way that is driven by God's Spirit, you don't ever want to go back to the easy and comfortable. People need to experience Spirit-empowered living so that during those times when they do feel lazy, they'll remember they have tasted and seen that he is good.

> The death of my parents caused me to have to live by faith and expect that God *would* answer my prayers.

My mother died when I was born. My father died when I was just twelve. God had a plan for me from the day he created me. He wanted me to live with an eternal perspective, so he had me deal with death at an early age. This set me on a path of living for eternity by making the most of today. He showed me that I am not guaranteed tomorrow—nor is anyone around me. And that allowed me to see beyond much of the comfort-driven desires that press all around us and, instead, ask God's Spirit to direct my life. The death of my parents caused me to have to live by faith and expect that God *would* answer my prayers. And every time he has, it just made my faith even stronger for the next time.

I came to see God as my dad. All things come from him. It would be crazy to ask my daughter how she got so many nice clothes. Of course, I paid for them. Sure, she could tell you which malls she went to and who went with her. But ultimately, all the stuff she has comes from me.

I really do look on my situation (to be able to lose this much and have to depend on God) as a blessing. From a very early age I understood that it's not about this life and it's silly to set yourself up for only this time on earth. James 4:14 says that our lives are just a mist—they can be over at any moment.

Second Corinthians 1:3-7 shows us how God comforts us in difficult times in order that we can pass on that comfort to others. To spend my childhood having no relationship with my dad prepared me for a world full of people who have no relationships with their fathers. It also prepared me for fatherhood. We can learn from both the successes and failures of those who have gone before us. I thank God for the positive lessons I learned from my parents but also for the negative examples I learned to avoid. Their sudden deaths have caused me to cherish every night with my children, not assuming that tomorrow will come. I tend to make the most of every opportunity.

It's weird how many people don't live by faith. I realize that others may not have had to live on their own, and may have had family support, and may not have had to depend solely on God. Maybe they haven't had the opportunity to live by faith and see God answer their prayers. From an early age, it was ingrained in me that it is not about our time on earth. We should spend our time for eternity and set ourselves up not for this present life but for the future. God wants us to be actively pursuing him now and for eternity.

Potential or Kinetic?

Kinetic energy is the energy of motion. It is the "energy contained by a form of matter because of its motion, or work that is needed to accelerate an object from rest to action."[1] It exists whenever an object or person has motion, such as a thrown baseball, an icicle falling to the ground, a dog barking, or a person walking. When matter is not in motion, it contains *potential energy,* which is essentially the opposite of kinetic energy. Potential energy transfers into kinetic energy when some kind of force is applied to the object to cause it to move in some way. Kinetic energy occurs when potential energy becomes unleashed; that is, when it is used, when it is exerted.

When I speak about kinetic energy in a spiritual sense, I am referring to the movement of the Holy Spirit prompting his people to action. I want to be led by him and empowered by him, so personal kinetic energy comes from spending time with him.

Lots of people wondered why Lisa and I decided to move on from Cornerstone Church, where I was pastor for sixteen years. The elders of Cornerstone and I felt that if true ministry is taking place, then it will keep going. It shouldn't have to be propped up by my teaching. If the Holy Spirit has moved and empowered others—if it's really of God—then the ministry should go on. It's almost a test to see if it really is kinetic and if the fruit that was born is real fruit. Jesus said in John 15:16, "I chose you and appointed you so that you might go and bear fruit—fruit that will last."

When I speak about kinetic energy in a spiritual sense, I am referring to the movement of the Holy Spirit prompting his people to action.

After I resigned from the church because I felt God was calling me elsewhere, it was very exciting to see the church members rally and come together. The church has shown itself to have a life of its own, a life that is of God.

When God unleashed the church on the Day of Pentecost (Acts 2),

unleashed

he infused a handful of simple, untrained, Galilean fishermen with his Spirit, and turned them into a dynamic force that would turn the world upside down. He taught the disciples how to make disciples—which is the primary function of a disciple.

What does that look like today? It's still about disciples of Jesus making other disciples. Once set in motion, the church is a force that will continue until Jesus returns. The true church is kinetic when discipleship of believers is the main focus. Without this focus of making disciples, the church would slowly die—and kinetic energy would only remain as potential energy.

> What does that look like today? It's still about disciples of Jesus making other disciples. Once set in motion, the church is a force that will continue until Jesus returns.

Which kind of energy characterizes your spiritual life?

Succumbing to Doubt or Leading by Faith?

In Acts 13 the apostle Paul and his faithful companion Barnabas traveled to a place called Pisidian Antioch, which is in the southern region of Galatia (modern-day Turkey). As was his custom, Paul headed toward the synagogue to share the good news about Jesus with the Jews and God-believing Gentiles who had gathered there. He recounted history from the days of Moses until the resurrection of the Christ. He proclaimed that Jesus' forgiveness was available for all sinners, both Jews and Gentiles. Then he quoted from the Old Testament prophet Habakkuk, "Look, you scoffers, wonder and perish, for I am going to do something in your days that you would never believe, even if someone told you" (Acts 13:41). Paul introduced this thought by pleading with the crowd to not let this happen to them—to not doubt what God could do and wanted to do in their midst.

unleashed

What doubts and roadblocks have we put in the way that have hindered the kinetic power of the Holy Spirit from doing what he wants to do in the church today as he did in the first-century church? How have we *not* demonstrated faith as leaders? Too often leaders of the church don't believe that God will do huge things through them. Or we don't believe God can do great things through the members of his church.

Late last year I spent time listening to the book of Genesis on CD. When you read about Jacob, you might think, *Man, he was an idiot. So was Abraham* . . . They were normal people who made some really dumb mistakes and poor choices, and yet they had faith. The point of the Scriptures is not that we would look at these guys and say, "OK, these guys are saints." The point is that they were just a bunch of ordinary guys who were as scared as we are, but they had faith in God and he came through for them. I wonder how many of us today walk around with that kind of faith.

If a person has been attending a church (assuming it's a Bible-teaching church) for the past two or three years, then he has more biblical information than a lot of pastors in India do. Yet churches in India are going out and changing their world. Many churchgoers lack courage and faith and think they don't know enough to disciple others. The truth is that today the church is flourishing in places where people have been exposed to a lot less biblical truth than we have in the American church. This doesn't mean we should not keep studying the Bible; it just proves to us that lack of knowledge cannot be an excuse.

Missionaries in Asia supported by Gospel for Asia are planting seventeen churches a day.[2] I can't even fathom seventeen a day. At the end of last year I traveled to India with my family to visit my friend K. P. Yohannan, founder and president of Gospel for Asia. I wanted to see in person how such things happen, especially in places like China, where the church has multiplied exponentially. After spending a couple of months in Asia, I discovered the "secret." It is not that the people are unusually talented or gifted; it has to do with their basic understanding of Scripture and Christianity. They are taught from the outset of their salvation that they are to spread the good news and make disciples. While we are taught to *memorize* the Great Commission, they are taught to actually *do* it. They take the Bible literally and live to make disciples. They also believe that the Holy Spirit will empower them as they go! There are still the normal human fears, but there is also a confidence, a dependence on God, and an attitude of "I don't really have a choice! God has spoken!"

It comes down to simple obedience, just being available to listen to what God wants to do with us.

I remember a time when I was not looking forward to cleaning out my garage. I knew it was going to take at least two or three hours, because my garage was just awful. (We do things like cleaning the garage only because we have to.) I remem-

> I was in the car with the driver less than two minutes when he started bawling his eyes out, as he started to tell me about his wife leaving him.

ber praying, "God, I don't want to spend this time on something that has zero eternal significance. Make this eternal somehow, because I just don't want to waste any time on this earth."

Then immediately, a neighbor I had been trying to talk to came over crying, needing to talk to me. I thought that was pretty awesome.

Another time I was in Colorado and needed a rental car. I found Enterprise in the yellow pages, called, and they said a guy would be out to pick me up in about fifteen minutes. I hung up the phone, and it occurred to me to ask, "God, make this of you." I'm not exaggerating when I tell you that I was in the car with the driver less than two minutes when he started bawling his eyes out, as he started to tell me about his wife leaving him. Later in the week I took him out for coffee and took him

unleashed

to a church nearby to try to get him plugged in there. I love when things like that happen.

One time a buddy of mine was going to leave his wife and run off with another girl. People had repeatedly tried to talk him out of it. They had written him letters, had done everything they could think of . . . but he was just done. He had his mind made up, but we were going to get together and talk one more time.

Before I met with him, I prayed, "God, just make it supernatural. It's got to be your Spirit. No one has been able to talk sense into him, but you can grab hold of him."

> People want to know that their lives are set up for as long as possible. We've practically made security into a virtue.

When we got together, we had just talked for a couple of minutes, when he said, "OK, I get it. I don't even know what you said. I can't tell you a thing you said, but for some reason, every single thing makes sense right now. It is clear in my mind, and I know what I have to do."

I asked him, "Nothing? You don't remember *anything* I said?"

"Nope," he replied. "But I know exactly what I need to do now."

When our churches start church plants, and when we send out missionaries, we must be confident that they will succeed in the power of the Spirit. We must not doubt but believe that God will do what he says he will do. Many people are afraid to just take God at his Word, obey him, and take risks, because *everything* in our culture is about security.

From the time that people are twenty-five years old, they are already worried about their retirement. They want to know, "What's going to happen to me forty years from now?" They want to know what's going to be happening until they die. The thought of doing anything without knowing the next step is ludicrous to people. They look at a lot of people in Scripture and think they were crazy. Like Abraham. Leave without a plan for the rest of your life? They think that Paul was foolish. Just go from city to city and not know what's next, just be led by the Spirit?

People want to know that their lives are set up for as long as possible. We've practically made security into a virtue, that it's the right thing to do. If you can set yourself up for the next ten years, and know you're secure, do it; if you can do it for twenty, do it; if you can even get enough money so that your kids don't have to work, and you can pay for their college, and get them set up in a house, do that. If you can even set it up so that your grandkids don't have to work, that's *really* virtuous. Everyone is set, and no one has to worry about a thing.

Yet people don't grow that way! The church needs more faith. That's what it comes down to. But many people don't like it when Jesus says, "Do not worry about your life, what you will eat or drink; or about your body, what you will wear" (Matthew 6:25). They want to set their lives up for the future.

What do we do that requires any faith? Many churchgoers don't do anything by faith, and often their lives just look the same as unbelievers' lives. They're really setting their lives up so they don't have to depend on God.

I've seen God do some incredible things. At one point in the life of Cornerstone, we made the decision to give half of our income away. It was amazing to see how much money came in. When we became aware of Children's Hunger Fund, the elders felt led to give them $1 million over the course of the year. We told them we'd send $250,000 every three months. Once, right after summer when the money came due, we had very little in the bank; but no one really knew about this problem. The check was due the next week, and I'm sure we could have called and said, "We're sorry, but the money didn't come in." But we had made a financial commitment. I chose not to tell anyone. No one knew when the check was due except for the finance department.

unleashed

The offering was taken that Sunday. When the finance team came into my office, they said, "You're not going to believe our offering."

I asked, "Why?"

They told me the figure was $251,000. That's crazy, because on average the offering received in those days was about $80,000. That's no coincidence. I asked them to leave, closed the door, and just started crying.

My whole life I had experienced that kind of thing, but this time I had needed to trust and see if God would do this sort of thing for the whole church. I had said, "God, I *know* that you love me, I know you take care of me, I know you always provide for me and have done so many things for me. But will I trust you to do the same with other people?" That was a lot scarier for me. I could deal with my own money because I've seen him answer my prayers numerous times, but now I was talking about thousands of people. And so when God responded in that huge way, and I knew it couldn't have been a coincidence, I just lost it.

Talking or Listening?

Some of my most intimate moments with God have occurred when I sensed his presence with me while sharing my faith, preaching, or doing things in his name. That's when I've felt like I've heard from him and was being led by him. Being kinetic is not sitting and waiting. It's in moving and ministering, I think, that God continues to speak and lead us—even through our mistakes. Look at the book of Acts. Paul started heading a certain direction, and God said more than once to him, "That's not where I want you to go" (see Acts 16:6, 7 for example). Often I have felt that I've been talking too much and not listening and obeying enough.

Sometimes in ministry we get so busy *doing* that we miss the power (the Holy Spirit) behind our busyness. We can avoid that by spending time alone with him, practicing an active prayer life throughout the day.

For way too many years in my ministry, I spent most of my energy on building a dynamic church service, rather than on listening to God and then obeying his directives.

When we decided to obey the promptings of the Holy Spirit and head toward Asia, not everyone understood, because we didn't have a detailed plan. We knew that we wanted to study some of the churches in Asia to learn more about the kids who are being trafficked in the sex trade, to learn more about the underground church, and to encourage the persecuted believers and the families of the martyrs. We believed that God was going to teach us through other heroes in the faith. But what this all meant for us, nobody—most of all, my wife and me—knew.

> When we decided to obey the promptings of the Holy Spirit and head toward Asia, not everyone understood, because we didn't have a detailed plan.

Sometimes we assume that we just have to climb to a mountaintop in order to experience the Holy Spirit and hear from him. Certainly there are times when we do need to get away and be quiet, and I pursue that discipline in my life . . . but we forget that the Holy Spirit also comes when we are in danger. Jesus promised his followers that he would give them words to say when they were brought before governing authorities (Luke 12:11, 12). When you look in the Scripture, it's when people were living lives that were not safe and doing things that steered them in the wrong direction that you see God responding. Those are the most intimate experiences—when God actually did something because the people involved needed him to do something . . . when they were in a situation and God unleashed his power.

God has shown our family over and over again that he walks with us. I can tell so many stories of his supernatural provision. It's all because of his grace. When I read about Joshua and Caleb, that they were the only

unleashed

ones who believed God could deliver the nation of Israel (Numbers 13, 14), it's a great reminder for me, whenever I encounter fear or uncertainty, to look back at all that God has done in my life. In the midst of the Joshua and Caleb episode, God asked Moses, "How long will these people treat me with contempt? How long will they refuse to believe in me, in spite of all the signs I have performed among them?" (Numbers 14:11).

We must learn to talk less and listen more.

Busyness or Discipleship?

The way many churches are set up today forces pastors to be busy in so many areas. It keeps them from personal prayer, from gathering believers to pray, and from expecting the supernatural to happen. Part of my going away was to see firsthand how the church flourishes when it takes on a different form than I've seen in America. Churches are closing their doors every day, and yet we're trying to maintain a system that we've created, because it's the easiest for the average churchgoer: he can go to church and his kids are taken care of, his teens are taken care of, and everything is provided for him. The paid staff will even lead his friends to the Lord and disciple them for him. Churchgoers may be tempted to think, *I'll just write a check and all my spiritual needs will be taken care of.* This church system keeps us busy *doing things,* but it also keeps people from really stepping out in faith, from taking responsibility and discipling people like they ought to. They expect pastors to do it all for them.

When most pastors I know first fell in love with Jesus, they just started sharing their faith with their friends, and then thought they wanted to

> Churchgoers may be tempted to think, *I'll just write a check and all my spiritual needs will be taken care of.*

do this for the rest of their lives. But then they got into church ministry and realized, *Some of this stuff is actually keeping me from doing the things that I love.* Pretty soon the pastors aren't sharing their faith anymore with the people they meet on the street or at the gym, and they're not discipling those they've led to the Lord. They're no longer setting an example for the people in their congregations.

If you look at other places in the world where the church is flourishing, it's because there isn't so much structure. It's about simplicity and about each person really believing the Spirit is in them, empowering them to go out and make more disciples.

> Pretty soon the pastors aren't sharing their faith anymore with the people they meet on the street or at the gym.

When I got involved with the church, I never thought I would fit in with the majority of people. I always thought I was doomed to be labeled as the extremist who ran too far ahead of the pack. As more people began looking at my life through a biblical lens rather than through an American one, they saw me as quite normal. The elders of the church not only accepted my actions as normal and exemplary, they started running ahead of me and challenging me to run faster. Newer believers were trained under godly men who expected them to love like disciples and surrender their lives—and people responded.

How do we know that we as leaders have done our job? It's when we see true commitment that is of the Spirit. It's when people are following the Spirit on their own rather than simply doing what the pastor tells them to do.

The church should be filled with laypeople creating their own gatherings in their own homes, leading people to the Lord, and teaching one another how to study the Word of God. Look back at Acts 13:

- Paul and Barnabas had to first "speak the word of God" (v. 46).
- The Gentiles "honored the word of the Lord" (v. 48).
- "The word of the Lord spread through the whole region" (v. 49).

There was kinetic power in the first-century church because the Word of the Lord was central to the teaching and sharing. In the New Testament we see a lot of people sharing their faith. And at Cornerstone it was thrilling to witness people gathering together in their houses and teaching one another how to make disciples. It can be a slow process, because it takes time to build disciples.

In Acts 13, they spoke the Word of the Lord both publicly and privately. After Paul spoke to those in the synagogue, the people invited Paul and Barnabas to speak further. A week later, on the Sabbath, "almost the whole city gathered to hear the word of the Lord. When the Jews saw the crowds, they were filled with jealousy. They began to contradict what Paul was saying and heaped abuse on him" (vv. 44, 45).

Likewise, today in the church the message of Jesus is sometimes accepted and praised and sometimes rejected. Many will applaud a sermon as long as they don't have to do anything about it. In our day, as in Paul's, a simple message of discipleship to Jesus is offensive to some people. When they are personally challenged to actually make disciples themselves, that's when resistance, frustration, and sometimes even anger arise. The thought is, *I like the old way when I didn't have to disciple and you did it for me. Why don't you keep doing it that way?*

In my opinion, the vast majority of those who go to church on Sunday morning do not want to make disciples; they rebel against it. The fact is that everyone should be making disciples, sharing their faith, and teaching others to obey God in everything he commanded (Matthew 28:19, 20). Many people can "Amen!" it in a sermon, but when a church leader says, "We're not going to do this program anymore.

We want you to actually share with your friends," that's when the criticism comes.

As a parent, my job is to teach my kids how to mature—so that when they grow up and leave my house, they won't need me so much. They'll be able to follow Jesus on their own. Sure, they are going to have some struggles, but they have to learn to make it in the real world themselves. I'm supposed to train my kids well enough so that I can release them into the world and they can go live the way they have been taught to live, and then help teach others how to live.

In the church, we are each supposed to entrust things to "reliable people who will also be qualified to teach others" (2 Timothy 2:2). That's discipleship, not busyness. It's a slow process, but the fruit that it bears will last.

Cowering in Fear or Praying for Boldness?

When my wife, Lisa, and I sold our home, packed up our stuff, and decided to head to Asia for two months or more with our four kids—ages fifteen, eleven, six, and five at the time—many people thought we were crazy. We were just trying to be obedient to God's call on our lives to live by faith. We believed that God would make it clear where we were supposed to settle down, when and if the time came. That isn't to say that we both didn't have times of uneasiness and fear. But we were at peace with this. Lisa asked me, "Why do people think it is so strange that we don't know what our next step is? It seems like there are so many people in Scripture who lived that way. Why is it so unbelievable that he would lead us to do the same?"

Fear of the unknown can really get its grip on us, can't it? But God asks us to seek him, trust him, and act. In Acts 13, after the Jews hurled their abuses at Paul and Barnabas, those two didn't cower in fear. Just the opposite. They "answered them boldly: 'We had to speak the word of God to you first. Since you reject it and do not consider yourselves worthy of eternal life, we now turn to the Gentiles'" (v. 46).

Paul was never accused of pulling any punches. He virtually had no filter. As was his custom in other cities that he visited, Paul first shared the message of Jesus' death and resurrection with the Jews before taking it the Gentiles. But since the Jews here rejected this message, Paul moved on. He was bold in his response to the Jews because he had prayed for boldness.

> The moment Peter and John were released from prison, they got together with the other believers and prayed for greater boldness.

In the early church we see the believers pray for boldness a lot. In Acts 4:13, the members of the Sanhedrin were astonished by the boldness of Peter and John. They realized that these followers of Jesus were just not going to back down. The moment Peter and John were released from prison, they got together with the other believers and prayed for greater boldness. Sure enough, the whole place where they were meeting started shaking; they left, and they preached more boldly (v. 31).

In Philippians 1:27, 28, Paul said, "Whatever happens, conduct yourselves in a manner worthy of the gospel of Christ. Then, whether I come and see you or only hear about you in my absence, I will know that you stand firm in the one Spirit, striving together as one for the faith of the gospel without being frightened in any way by those who oppose you. This is a sign to them that they will be destroyed, but that you will be saved—and that by God."

Did you catch that phrase: "without being frightened in any way"? Unless we're bold, the world will not believe. Many people in the church are scared to share their faith and don't believe they can. Where's the courage? I read in Scripture that the early church got together regularly in their homes and prayed specifically for courage. It's more about praying for boldness than anything else. But today we don't pray like that. Too often we pray:

- "Oh, my aunt is sick. Pray for her."
- "I don't feel good . . . pray for me. I'm depressed."
- "Make me more comfortable."

Too many of our prayer requests are all about *me*. I don't want to sound cynical. Of course, we need to do some of that kind of praying. We just don't realize how strong the desire for comfort is in our culture. And this is the stuff that gets in the way of our being kinetic. Instead, we should be praying for boldness in our churches and in our individual lives. Where are believers getting together, wanting to be bold so badly that the whole place is shaking?

> Where are believers getting together, wanting to be bold so badly that the whole place is shaking?

Last fall I started praying with some college guys for boldness and courage. When they leave those meetings, they are bolder because that's what we prayed for. We need to learn how to truly fellowship. It doesn't mean a potluck and playing church softball together. It's getting together and saying, "You need to get out there and share your faith, and I'm going to pray for you every day, that God gives you opportunities and makes you more bold. Next week I'm going to ask you about your boldness and whether or not you did something. I know you're scared about this. I'm scared too. I need you to stick with me. If you don't help me out, I'm just going to get lazy again and go hang out, play golf, whatever. I need you to push me."

unleashed

In the church we need to push each other that way. The author of Hebrews challenged us, "Let us consider how we may spur one another on toward love and good deeds" (10:24). The early believers did that. In the midst of persecution and threats (see Acts 13:50-52), the church did not slow down. It actually picked up steam. That's because persecution gets you serious. It gets you to think through your commitment to Jesus. The lukewarm quickly back off, which enables true fellowship to take place among those who are serious about their faith. Persecution also takes our minds off our comfort, our personal pleasure; and it forces us to a closer dependence on our Father. Fear is of the enemy, but boldness is of God.

Looking Back or Moving Forward?

I love the ending to chapter 13 of Acts: "And the disciples were filled with joy and with the Holy Spirit" (v. 52). The truth of the message of Jesus had been shared with Jews and Gentiles alike. There had been some persecution, but the Word of God spread through the whole region where Paul and Barnabas were. And many people believed. In the midst of some tests and trials, the Holy Spirit filled the disciples with his deep joy. He asks us to do our part in obedience, and he will be faithful to do his.

We must believe the words of Scripture. My favorite verse is James 5:17, "Elijah was a human being, even as we are. He prayed earnestly that it would not rain, and it did not rain on the land for three and a half years." This is having kinetic, Spirit-led faith. And I want that kind of faith; I want to believe that I have surrendered my life to the will of God, allowing him to lead my family and me to any place on the earth. I pray he shows me any areas of my life that I have not truly surrendered. I pray that I would know him more deeply, experience his power more fully, and minister more effectively than ever. We are just human beings like Elijah, but we can pray and believe earnestly.

We must trust the Holy Spirit to empower the lives of those in our congregations. We must believe that he can take an average guy and inspire him to actually lead his neighborhood to the Lord. God used a dozen or so ordinary men to get the message to the whole world (eleven of the original twelve apostles, Matthias—who replaced Judas Iscariot, and Paul.) In the church of the future, leaders need to look at their members and say (like we do to our kids): "You're just here for a little while, but we've got to kick you out at some point. You've got to start making your own disciples. You need to live your own life. I will always be here cheering you on, loving you, giving advice when you need it. That will never change. But you don't need me like you did when you were young. Go for it. Go do your thing." We must work on releasing people for ministry, and trusting that the Holy Spirit can do great things through ordinary people.

> We must work on releasing people for ministry, and trusting that the Holy Spirit can do great things through ordinary people.

People have told me for years that the things that happen in the church overseas could never happen in the U.S.—that people here are just too materialistic, they're not as committed, they like the big show, they like the numbers . . . people won't come if it's only a bunch of people praying in a room. People say that overseas they're more into relationships, more into family.

And you know what? I just don't buy that. I'm not ready to give up on the church in America like that. I see many in the younger generation who look at their parents' religion and say, "They don't get it." These young people are so disinterested with all that they see. They don't like the lack of commitment, and they're not thrilled with their parents' religion because they never really saw God do anything great in their homes. They've seen their parents go to church and Bible studies, and not swear, but have they seen them *experience God?* We have a younger generation that's saying, "Just give me what's biblical. I want to see God do supernatural things in my life and empower me with his Spirit, or I don't want to have anything to do with it. I don't want to just attend another church program or drama or outreach; I want to see the Holy Spirit move. I want the real thing."

Now there are exceptions to this. Obviously, there are some older believers still living by faith. And there are many young people who are caught up in the pursuit of comfort. In general, though, the younger generation is crying out for something more.

So what are we going to do about it? I'd like to give them the real thing: the church unleashed in all its kinetic power, driven by a mighty move of the Holy Spirit. I am praying boldly for this. Will you join me?

unequivocal

Acts 20:22-24

I don't understand what you are saying."

It was a poor choice of words, I found. The tech-support guy on the other end of the phone assumed I was hard of hearing.

He spoke louder. "I said that the software system is asynchronous and is not designed to accomplish automatic archiving of any SMS data. Our company policies prohibit me from addressing any work-arounds that involve outside decryption of the PB files."

"Look, Michael," I said, aiming for a patient tone and reminding myself that when he became the third technician I was transferred to nearly thirty long minutes ago, I had told him I was a minister. "I just want to get my text messages back. They told me when I got this new phone that all my stuff would be transferred."

"Sir, *stuff* is not a word any of our people would have used."

This was getting worse and I was getting tired. The joy of owning a new smart phone had quickly given way to the frustration of losing at least a hundred important text messages with phone numbers and dates of meetings and . . . you get the picture. So I pulled the ultimate take-me-up-the-chain card.

"Can I speak to a supervisor?"

There was a relieved sigh, and he said "Gladly!" just a little too gladly.

Two minutes of on-hold music later, a female voice said, "Hi, I'm Jane, technical support supervisor. How can I help you?"

Starting from the beginning—again—I told the story of my new phone and all I had been promised and how I had gone back three times to see if they could get all my old data, and about the young guy with the goatee at the store who told me they had this secret program that could actually get the *stuff* back—but it was complicated—and that he had said, "You'll need some real good tech help and—"

"Sir, may I say something?" she asked, stopping me mid-sentence.

"Sure. Go for it."

> Sometimes we'd rather people would speak peace and prosperity even if it's not quite true, because then we can sleep at night.

"Your text messages are gone. They are toast. Shredded. Vanished. Absolutely deleted. They have gone to the Land of Lost Things, and you will never see any of them again." I was stunned into silence. "Sir, are you still there?"

"Yeah . . . and thank you very much."

It was her turn to be stunned. "Why are you thanking me? I normally get cussed out at this point."

"Because I finally met somebody who would simply tell me the truth. So thank you . . . and have a nice day!"

Ever been there?

If you've ever wanted someone to just shoot straight with you and spare you the spin, if you've ever begged a friend to cut the blather and tell you the bold-faced truth, if you've ever hoped that a doctor or lawyer or preacher would just break it down without sugarcoating it, then you understand the need for the gift of the truth.

It is a priceless gift, one that frees us to face our situations with certainty and clarity. But like most precious things, hearing the truth comes at a cost. We may have to surrender some naive notions that were giving us a false but comforting sense of peace. In fact, the gift of truth is sometimes gladly exchanged for the gift of tranquility. As the old song goes, "Tell me something good!" Sometimes we'd rather people would speak peace and prosperity even if it's not quite true, because then we can sleep at night. That's why some folks are furious that WikiLeaks and organizations like it publish secret documents. They would rather not know the truth and be comfy. But if it's really not a matter of national security, wouldn't you rather know the facts than sleep with a lie?

Telling the Truth

And that brings us to my favorite apostle, Paul. (I think I'm more like Peter, but when I grow up I want to be like Paul.) This reformed Christian-killer made truth telling an art. Once God had knocked him off his high horse on the Damascus road, Paul became a poster boy for my grandma's favorite phrase: "Tell the truth and shame the devil!"

Paul told the truth about how messed up mankind is and how Jesus is the answer (see the book of Romans). He told the truth about what it costs to follow Christ (see Philippians). He told the truth about how trusting Christ should change the way we treat others (see Philemon). He was clear that trusting anything other than Christ, including our own goodness, is a dead-end journey (see Galatians). He even told the truth about what a jerk he was and how God would still accept an arrogant, flawed, loudmouthed man as an evangelist (see my life . . . and 1 Corinthians 15:9, 10: "I am the least of the apostles and do not even deserve to be called an apostle, because I persecuted the church of God. But by the grace of God I am what I am, and his grace to me was not without effect. No, I worked harder than all of them—yet not I, but the grace of God that was with me").

Paul was a truth teller, but that doesn't mean he always *knew* the truth. Like the rest of us, he had moments when he knew in part but not in whole. Take the moment at the seashore with his good friends, the church leaders from Ephesus. Luke described this tender scene with love and pain. Paul and his friends wept at the possibility that this might be their last chat this side of eternity (Acts 20:37, 38). The Ephesian elders' father in the faith was heading for the last mile. And

unleashed

as he did, he walked them down memory lane, reminding them of his faithful ministry in their city and pouring out his heart with passionate warnings and words of advice. Right in the middle of this long good-bye, he confessed an important fact: "And now, compelled by the Spirit, I am going to Jerusalem, not knowing what will happen to me there" (v. 22).

Paul was not afraid to tell the truth, even when he didn't *know* the truth! He knew from the Spirit's warnings that when he got to Jerusalem, receiving the key to the city probably wasn't on the itinerary. Every believer in the early church knew that Jerusalem was not a hospitable place for followers of Christ. It had been the epicenter of the wave of persecution that Paul himself had helped to launch—a wave that evangelists and preachers had ridden out of that town so that they could take the gospel into all the world. All this he knew, yet he was unequivocal about his plans: "I am going to Jerusalem." There are some wonderful clues to his unequivocal vision in these few words.

> Paul was not afraid to tell the truth, even when he didn't *know* the truth!

I Am Going . . . but I Don't Really Want To!

It's worth noting that going to Jerusalem may not have been Paul's first choice. I have a tendency to think that he was stoically determined to head to the city of David. But his words reveal the pressure behind the journey: "And now, compelled by the Spirit, I am going . . ." The tip-off is in the word he used to describe this compelling feeling. It is *deo,* a Greek word meaning to "bind" or "tie up."[1] It's the same word Luke used one chapter later when it was predicted that Paul would be "bound" hand and foot by the Jewish leaders in Jerusalem (Acts 21:13). Not a comfy word choice—but a telling one. Perhaps the apostle didn't really want to go, but he felt *bound* to. Obligation and commitment are not popular topics today. From cell phone contracts to marriage certificates to long-term church commitments, we live in a society that hates to be bound to anything. If something better comes along, we often want out with a "no early termination penalty."

But Paul charted a different course. I'm actually not sure that the spirit he was speaking of is the Holy Spirit. Before you brand me a heretic, look at how the *King James Version* translates Acts 20:22: "And now, behold, I go *bound in the spirit* unto Jerusalem, not knowing the things that shall befall me there" (emphasis added). Paul may simply have been saying, "I'm just tied to the belief that going to Jerusalem is what I ought to do—even if I don't want to do it."

That's a concept I've tried hard to get my sons to understand: doing the right thing even when you don't want to! An old friend of mine used to say, "Most of the greatest things in the world were accomplished by people who didn't want to do them." I dare you to put that on a note and post it on your teenager's bathroom mirror! There is great strength and value in turning a deaf ear to my body's complaints in order to stick with my integrity's call. It is the core of Christ's call to sacrifice. Just as Jesus suffered and did what he didn't want to do on Calvary (see Mark 14:36), we are called to deny ourselves that others might benefit. That's a lesson worth posting in church leadership meeting rooms as well.

I will be the first to confess that too much of my energy gets siphoned away in an effort to make church folks happy. If the worship isn't passionate enough or the sermon powerful enough, I'm stressed out that somebody is going to be checking out the new church down the street. More than one church leader has thought something like this: *If we'll just make becoming a Christian a bit more convenient, I bet we could up our numbers by 13 percent!*

Following Christ must not be graded on a comfort scale. We are bound to teach the truth of the Jesus who loved the prostitute and the Pharisee with the same heart. He is the same Jesus who was comfortable not only eating with the tax collector but also receiving the scorn of the religious elite. The bottom line is this: Lazy Boy doesn't manufacture a line of crosses. The humble path of the carpenter King was unequivocally set on doing the right thing . . . even when it meant death. And that is where Paul had his heading set as well: *I am going to Jerusalem.*

So whether your "Jerusalem" is being faithful in raising a disabled child or staying the course through a tough time in ministry, an unequivocal commitment to do the right thing is priceless. Yours might be telling the truth when lying would be so much easier, or walking with a loved one through the throes of cancer or Alzheimer's. These are the choices that reveal character and expose the work of God in our hearts. They are not fun, but they are fundamental. So whenever you are "bound in the spirit" to do a hard thing—because it is the right thing, the thing God has given you to do—know that you are walking shoulder to shoulder with Paul on the dusty road whose end is our own Jerusalem.

> We are bound to teach the truth of the Jesus who loved the prostitute and the Pharisee with the same heart.

I Know *Some* Things . . . but I Don't Know It All!

There's another gem in this passage of Scripture. While Paul was unequivocal about the direction of his trip, he was willing to admit that he wasn't certain of its outcome. He said, "I am going to Jerusalem, not knowing what will happen to me there. I only know that in every city the Holy Spirit warns me that prison and hardships are facing me" (Acts 20:22, 23). Yes, this trip looked like a last march for the gospel soldier, but he couldn't be sure—so he didn't say he was.

Did you catch that? This inspired apostle purposely *held back* from declaring what he didn't know for certain. Here's a little advice that we who would follow in his footsteps might profit from: don't preach what you can't prove!

It's so tempting to make proclamations that are way above our pay grade. You know the ones:

- Which methods of honoring God will receive his approval and which won't!
- What translation of Christ's words Paul would use and which ones he would pass on!

> In the name of "standing for the truth," too many of us get lured into *stretching* the truth to where we think it should reach.

- Whose interpretation of Scripture gets God's thumbs-up and who is simply washed up!
- Whose last-days time line is solid and whose is just plain stupid!
- Who is bound for glory and who's gonna roast!

In the name of "standing for the truth," too many of us get lured into *stretching* the truth to where we think it should reach. I should know: I have been a pro at this. As a young preacher I scorched the pews with sermons that condemned everything from dancing to that glass of wine some "slippery slope liberals" were having with their dinners. And man, was I good! I could put you on a guilt trip that made an around-the-world cruise look like a paddleboat ride on a pond.

Some of my tirades went something like this: "If drunkenness is a sin, what's the best way to keep from ever getting drunk? Don't take a drink. Pretty simple, I think! So if you do take a drink, which drink will get you into sin? The third one? The fifth one? My friends, the devil doesn't want you to know it, but it was the *first one!*"

unleashed

I just have to stop and say that if any of my old parishioners are reading this, please accept my apologies! I was so full of myself and thought I was really helping, but I was actually blurring the truth by embellishing it. I was speaking unequivocally about that which I didn't understand.

Funny, it's so hard to see this error when you are the one making it, but so easy to spot it when someone else is. Didn't Jesus say something about looking for a speck in your brother's eye while you have a plank in your own? One of my favorite "plank discovery moments" came because of number 37.

A couple of decades ago, I attended a large youth conference with a few thousand teens at a big civic center in the Midwest. When the invitation was offered on Friday night, God opened the floodgates. Over sixty teenagers came to be baptized into Christ. Well, those of us running the thing were caught a bit unprepared—oh, we of little faith—so we had to scramble to gather sufficient towels and baptismal garments for all these young believers.

We set up a makeshift baptistery on the stage with a curtained-off changing space for the kids offstage on both sides—but we had only eight baptismal gowns. Since we didn't want the teenagers to leave the conference in wet clothes, we did what we had to. As soon as one new Christian would get out of the water and take off his or her baptismal gown, we would wring it out, then race it around the other side to hand it off to the next penitent sinner. It was a holy Cirque du Soleil, if you will—with kids entering the tank from one side, going out the other, and wild-eyed youth workers joyfully running around the back of the stage, swapping wet gowns and high fives. We were stoked—in a very humble and godly manner, of course.

During one of these breathless runs, I was grabbed by a very agitated adult who had come out of the audience. "Excuse me, young man, but you have a problem." Now there was an astute observation! "Number 37 didn't go all the way under," he declared. "He's got to be baptized again!"

OK, let this sink in: I was standing there, holding a dripping gown and staring at this clearly obsessed fellow Christian while three thousand kids were singing one more verse of "I Have Decided to Follow Jesus" as they waited for the next baptism—which would take place in the nude if I didn't get this garment to the dressing booth on stage left immediately.

"Well?" he asked persistently. "What are you gonna do?"

Stunned, I went on autopilot. "Do you know the name of this kid? Is he from your church?" I asked, continuing to wring out the gown.

"No, I don't know him. But I was keeping a real good count, and I'm sure it was number 37. His arm didn't go all the way under the water." He said this last part in a whisper, like someone sharing the news of a good friend's terminal diagnosis.

Before my brain could stop my mouth, I asked, "Well, what was he wearing?"

The older man shifted his gaze to the gown I was wringing out, with a look that couldn't be called appreciative. I sighed, made a quick decision, and started heading on around to the changing booth.

"So what are you gonna do?" he hollered after me.

Over the strains of the old hymn, I yelled back, "Trust Jesus!" and disappeared around a curtain. Thankfully, the fellow must have given up, because when I made my next circuit he was gone. I've pondered often about the tension one must tolerate if things like that are what drive your faith. And lest you think I've lost every legalistic bone in *my* body, my greatest nightmare is meeting a one-armed kid in Heaven who introduces himself to me as number 37.

You see, knowing what to be unequivocal *about* is the key to the gospel.

• I must be unchanging when it comes to the power of God's grace and Christ's blood.

unleashed

- I cannot waver about the call to share the good news and to love my neighbor as myself.
- I dare not shift my feet from the solid rock of Christ's resurrection and promised return.

But there are a number of things about which I need to join Paul in saying, "I just don't know what all is going to happen." The problem, as I see it, is that God chose to hold certain cards close to his divine chest. For example, no matter how well you've got the book of Revelation figured out, don't start telling me when Jesus is coming back. You don't know . . . and neither do I. Jesus said so: "About that day or hour no one knows, not even the angels in heaven, nor the Son, but only the Father" (Matthew 24:36). Yet prognosticators have wrongly predicted different days and hours for years. God alone will separate the sheep from the goats and grant eternity to those who have trusted in his Son—and he alone knows when he will do this.

That's just one reason why he's God . . . and we're not!

If I Do Nothing Else . . . I'm Telling the Good News!

After telling the Ephesian leaders that he was heading to Jerusalem even though he didn't know all the circumstances, Paul made clear that none of the difficult, known facts nor divine unknowns would deter him from his mission: sharing the love of Christ with a hurting world. First and foremost, his passionate priority was the advancement of the kingdom of Heaven. About that, he was the most unequivocally unequivocal: "I consider my life worth nothing to me; my only aim is to finish the race and complete the task the Lord Jesus has given me—the task of testifying to the good news of God's grace" (Acts 20:24).

Having already alluded to the high stakes of his journey, Paul put the big, bad *D* word front and center: DEATH. It had to be the unspoken question in the eyes of those close friends as they stood together on the seashore: *Are you going to be martyred, Paul?*

It's one thing to say that you are going to die. Hello. News flash. Everybody is going to die! As one old preacher said, "Nobody gets outta this life alive!" But martyrdom is another matter.

John Foxe devoted himself to gathering the stories of men and women throughout the centuries who paid the ultimate price for their faith. A quick review of their stories in *Foxe's Book of Martyrs* will remind you that the toughest time for martyrs isn't when they die. It's those last few minutes right beforehand that get you.

> Paul made clear that none of the difficult, known facts nor divine unknowns would deter him from his mission: sharing the love of Christ with a hurting world.

- It's when they first light the wood around the stake they have tied you to.
- It's when they drive in the first nail to hold you to the cross.
- It's when they begin to turn the lever on the rack that will stretch your limbs until they tear loose.

You get the picture. Well, actually, you don't. The vast majority of us never will. Our religious freedoms are fiercely guarded by our government. The police protect the sanctity of our worship assemblies, and the courts will defend our right to preach about Jesus every Sunday till he comes again—at least I hope so. For most of us, martyrs are mere black-and-white sketches we vaguely remember from church history classes—though Christians are still being martyred in our world today. So why were the martyrs of old so sure, while we are so often the opposite of unequivocal?

unleashed

Ask yourself, *What prompts us to soft-pedal the reality of eternity or to hide the truth of Jesus' coming judgment?* How do we end up swapping the profession of our faith for a project-of-the-month community service plan? Some answers put the blame on the corruption in our culture or the lure of luxury and wealth. But there's a starker truth lurking behind these clichés. Maybe we just *aren't that sure.* Oh, we'll sing and shout it with the best of them, but when it comes to laying down our time, our money, or our reputations . . . we equivocate, big time. This is a fancy way of saying we are afraid to commit ourselves—really commit ourselves—to the cause of Christ.

> How do we end up swapping the profession of our faith for a project-of-the-month community service plan?

Think I'm being too harsh? If every believer were to lead just one person to Christ this year, every church would double. (OK, math majors, I know some would die and some would fall away, but put your calculators down for a minute and just go with me.) How many churches will double this year? Not many. And if one church would do this a few years in a row, we would put them on the cover of *Outreach* magazine and invite the minister to speak at our conferences. And for what? For being what *should* be normal! Or rather, what *would* be normal if we allowed the Spirit to help us emulate Paul's attitude: "I consider my life worth nothing to me; my only aim is to finish the race and complete the task!"

The heart of the world's greatest missionary is staring us in the face. We each have to decide what is worth our lives. If gathering a few million pieces of paper we call dollars or garnering a few thousand friends on Facebook is what your life is worth, you may as well sell yourself on eBay. (By the way, that's been tried too.) But surely that small voice in your heart tells you that you are worth so much more. Surely you feel in your bones that your life is about something so much bigger than a house or career or bank account can contain.

We have been called to an eternal purpose: to share the best news the world has ever known. Nothing can compare with the value of this mission, nor can anything substitute for it. And when we see it lived out, we never forget it.

When Joy came walking into our church that Sunday four years ago, she would have been pretty easy to dismiss. Dressed a bit too provocatively and carrying a pretty-good-size chip on her shoulder, among her first words were, "I really don't care much for Christians." Her mother had dragged this thirtysomething to see me, and I'd invited her to worship with us. She appeared less like she was seeking Jesus and more like she was spoiling for a fight. There seemed to be such an intense pain in her heart.

And who could blame her? Her husband was in jail, and she was due in court over some pretty nasty accusations centering on their hobby. This young couple had gone so deep into the occult that they had set themselves up online as modern-day demon wranglers. And not the kind who throw *out* the demons, mind you. They were advertising on occult Web sites that they could show people how to get in league with Satan's minions and use them to get what was desired. I didn't even know such a thing existed. Talk about spooky!

As Joy shared bits of her story with folks at our church, one of them did a little Google search and sent me a link to a newspaper article about the trial. It was graphic, gross, and depressing. Joy's husband had been charged with several counts of abuse that had landed him in court. He

unleashed

was awaiting the trial, and bail was way more than they could think about paying. Joy was angry, bitter, and alternately wanted to beat someone up or bawl her eyes out. Needless to say, it made for some interesting lobby conversations on Sundays!

But Joy kept coming, and church people kept loving her and praying with her. They didn't let the publicity or the seedy side of her story offend them. They simply shared the good news of God's grace.

I remember the day that Joy decided to trust Christ and be baptized. "I'm so scared," she confided to me. "I just don't know what Joe will think when he finds out!" It seemed a pretty rational fear to me.

I reflected on how thrilled my parents were when I was baptized, and tried to imagine their reaction had the family's business been satanic demon coaching. *Displeased* would have been an understatement. But as God often does, he gave me the right words to say to her: "Why don't we just let God handle that one?"

Joy agreed and was baptized the next week. Over the following month we prayed for her husband's upcoming trial, and she began to drop some hints in letters to him of the changes she was going through. Imagine her trying to figure out how to write about this: "Hey, honey, how's everything in prison? Oh, by the way, you'll never guess what's happened to me . . ."

Then things changed. The original trial date was postponed, and the judge decided that Joe was less of a flight risk than he had first believed. We were all surprised the Sunday Joy announced that he was coming home that next week. How would he react to her commitment to Christ? We prayed like crazy, asking God to help her handle however Joe reacted. To be honest, my best-case scenario was that the guy would get angry and cut off contact with Joy. The last thing this new Christian needed was her Satan-worshipping husband pouring cold water on her infant faith.

But God had something else up his sleeve. When Joe came to church the next Sunday, he and Joy were all smiles. She had chosen to let Joe know about her baptism in a phone call before he got home. The amazing part was that when she told Joe about her new faith, he began to laugh. While in prison, someone had reached out to him with the gospel, and now he wanted to be baptized. He had actually been concerned about how *Joy* would react!

Needless to say, we had a great celebration! And—long story short—these two continue to be faithful examples at our church of what happens when believers unequivocally focus on the mission: sharing Jesus with whomever God puts in front of you! It is the one thing that will take you through life's ups and downs and even prepare you for the final curtain. When our life stories are over, what we have done with that mission—sharing the gospel of grace—is all that will matter.

> These two continue to be faithful examples at our church of what happens when believers unequivocally focus on the mission: sharing Jesus with whomever God puts in front of you!

And that's how you face the *D* word.

Unequivocally Sure

I buried my mother, Mildred Walling, three days after Christmas last year. It was tough, but it was wonderful. She had lived a faithful Christian life for nearly ninety-four years. Having been a Sunday school teacher and preacher's wife for most of her life, she was the kind of example every church wants and every child needs. I was blessed. (Just pull her name up on YouTube for a taste of this feisty little lady's faith and spirit as she recites 1 Corinthians 13 from memory at age ninety-two! Go ahead. I'll wait.)

unleashed

My siblings and I got to spend her last week with her in Southern California and thank her for all she had done. It was a holy privilege to hear her pray a prayer of thanksgiving for her life just forty-eight hours before she went home to her Lord and her husband. We held a beautiful memorial service and buried her next to my father. I flew home realizing that both my parents were gone—and missing them terribly.

But it was ten days after Mom's funeral that God let me more fully understand the secret to such faith.

Another friend at church had lost her grandmother and asked me to say a prayer at her funeral. This grandmother, a member at an African-American church in a nearby community, had also lived a long faithful life of Christian service. Though I had never met the lady, I agreed to take part in her service.

My wife and I arrived at the little church building several minutes before the funeral was to begin. To my dismay, I found out that the viewing of the body had taken place directly before the service, so the church was full and the other pastors taking part were already seated on the stage. I was quickly ushered to the front and placed up on the pulpit platform with the rest. It was about this time that I realized something: my wife, Cathryn, and I were the only Caucasians in the building. This was a black church, from the choir in the front to the ushers in the back. Now, that fact didn't make me uncomfortable. But being seated in full view of the whole church for the entire service was a bit much. There I was, still somewhat emotionally raw from my own mother's passing, and I was supposed to sit there through a service about a great Christian lady whom I had never met, and try to keep from bawling uncontrollably. I'm a crier, OK? I can't help it. But I didn't want to look like I was faking it. Who wanted some boohooing white guy from another church, plopped right in front of the grieving family, taking center stage with his tears at someone else's grandma's funeral? I was petrified.

But then worship started. And I do mean *worship*!

This was no hankie-blowing, sad song memorial. These folks really believed that Miss Betty had gone home, and they were gonna sing like it. The praise band had a hot saxophonist who knew how to play, and he led the way. An elderly lady in the choir did a solo called "God Is My All in All" that raised the roof. I was singing and swaying and clapping with the rest.

So when it came my time to pray, brother, I prayed! I mean, I just cut loose. I prayed the truth from my heart about Christ's victory over death and the promise we have of life eternal as if I were preaching at a revival. The band even started playing rhythmic hits between the sentences of my prayer, like something out of *Sister Act*. And that just fueled my fire. The church "Amened!" and "Oh yeahed!" as I prayed, and the band did a little flourish after my final amen. Some in the choir actually applauded. I sat down and nodded to the family, who were smiling kindly. I thought, somewhat smugly, *Bet they're glad that granddaughter goes to my church!*

> This was no hankie-blowing, sad song memorial. These folks really believed that Miss Betty had gone home, and they were gonna sing like it.

Then their pastor got up to speak. Well, I don't mean speak. I mean *preach*!

This guy started in about the great life Miss Betty had lived, but he hit second gear when he moved on to the great death she had died. Faithful to the last, she had been raising two great-grandsons, bringing them regularly to church. Her death was a testimony to her life and her Lord. But the pastor didn't quit there.

"We are all gonna die!" he thundered. "Old Death is gonna come knocking at your door . . . and yours and yours!" he said, as he pointed to various parishioners. Plenty of "Oh yeahs!" and "That's rights!" and even a few laughs could be heard.

"But when Death comes knocking on my door . . . I want to be like Miss Betty. I'm gonna say, 'Hello, Death! Come on in here! I been waiting on you. I ain't afraid of you. I ain't running from you. I know who you are—my Jesus has defeated you! You are just my chariot to Heaven!'"

> "I'm not afraid, because I know whom I have believed in and I know how to die: in Jesus Christ!"

The congregation roared—and so did I. And that just revved him up.

"Death, you are my cabbie to glory! . . . You are my chauffeur to Jesus! . . . You are my ride to the other side! I'm not afraid, because I know whom I have believed in and I know how to die: in Jesus Christ!"

Well, suffice to say that the place went up in flames! Praise songs and prayers mingled with "Hallelujahs!" and by the time the service was over, we fairly danced our way down the aisle in front of the casket.

As we got into the car, my wife turned to me and said, "That's the kind of funeral I want to have!"

Don't we all? And the way to have it is simple. A home-going celebration like that is for people who are *sure*. For when you are sure, you no longer count anything—even life itself—more precious than finishing the race and completing the task.

That's the kind of lives and deaths that will change our world.

That's the kind of faith that will move mountains and countries and kings.

That's the kind of faith that I pray God will breathe into you and me today and that the Spirit will blow on Old Death when it calls for us.

Because you can only live that way when you are sure.

Unequivocally sure.

| Conclusion |

I t's a fact. The first-century church turned the world upside down for the cause of Christ. The Holy Spirit of God unleashed the sold-out saints on their culture. They were a beautiful kaleidoscope comprised of diverse backgrounds and races with a cross section of all the gifts and talents needed to get the job done. As the Word of God spread, in spite of hazardous risks and persecution, the church's growth was kinetic and innumerable, creating pandemonium wherever Christians were present. The places they met, both publicly and from house to house, were shaken. The believers were lavish in their worship of God and in their generosity toward others. And their mission was unequivocal.

We're praying that as God unleashes his church on the world today, Christ's followers will imitate the passion of the first-century church, be infused with the power of the Holy Spirit, and be impelled to turn the world upside down for his glory.

Equipped with and inspired by the pages of Scripture, may you become a critical part of this movement—one that is sure to sweep across our country and our world to the glory of God and for the advancement of his kingdom. God's people can and will change the world. Are you ready?

| Notes |

Chapter 1

1. http://www.google.com/publicdata?ds=uspopulation&met=population& idim=state:06000&dl=en&hl=en&q=what+is+the+population+of+california.

2. http://en.wikipedia.org/wiki/List_of_U.S._states_by_population.

3. http://en.wikipedia.org/wiki/Proposition_8.

4. http://thesaurus.com/opt/Greek-Word-for-Power.

5. http://www.google.com/publicdata?ds=uspopulation&met=population& tdim=true&dl=en&hl=en&q=how+many+people+live+in+america%3F.

6. http://www.covenanteyes.com/2010/01/06/updated-pornography-statistics (accessed January 11, 2011).

7. http://www.nationalaffairs.com/publications/detail/the-evolution-of-divorce and http://www.aboutdivorce.org/us_divorce_rates.html (accessed January 11, 2011).

8. http://www.nrlc.org/abortion/facts/abortionstats.html (accessed January 11, 2011).

9. http://www.thetravelerszone.com/travel-destinations/top-25-most-visited-tourist-destinations-in-america/

10. The author did a comparison of the churches listed in California in the *Directory of the Ministry: A Yearbook of Christian Churches and Churches of Christ* from 1990 to 2000.

11. http://www.searchgodsword.org/lex/grk/view.cgi?number=4741.

12. Tom Minnery, *Why You Can't Stay Silent: A Biblical Mandate to Shape Our Culture* (Wheaton, IL: Tyndale House Publishers), 64–65.

13. Erwin W. Lutzer, *When a Nation Forgets God: 7 Lessons We Must Learn from Nazi Germany* (Chicago: Moody Publishers, 2010), 21–22.

Chapter 2

1. www.etymonline.com.

2. Martin Luther King Jr., http://www.wmich.edu/~ulib/archives/mlk/q-a.
html (accessed February 15, 2011).

3. Winfred E. Garrison and Alfred T. DeGroot, *The Disciples of Christ: A History* (St. Louis, MO: Christian Board of Publications, 1948), 468.

4. Lawrence A. Q. Burnley, *The Cost of Unity: African-American Agency and Education in the Christian Church, 1865–1914* (Macon, GA: Mercer University Press, 2008), 125.

Chapter 3

(All online sources in this chapter were accessed February 15, 2011.)

1. http://www.globalchange.umich.edu/globalchange2/current/lectures/
pop_socio/pop_socio.html

2. Ibid.

3. http://www.adherents.com/Religions_By_Adherents.html.

4. Rodney Stark, *Cities of God: The Real Story of How Christianity Became an Urban Movement and Conquered Rome* (New York: HarperCollins, 2006), 67.

5. David T. Olson, *The American Church in Crisis* (Grand Rapids, MI: Zondervan, 2008), 29–30.

6. http://www.wordiq.com/definition/ology.

7. http://users.tinyonline.co.uk/gswithenbank/ologies.htm.

8. I am deeply indebted to Alan Hirsch for his revolutionary insights on this subject. For further study read *The Shaping of Things to Come* by Michael Frost and Alan Hirsch, Hendrickson Publishers, 2003.

9. Michael Frost and Alan Hirsch, *The Shaping of Things to Come: Innovation and Mission for the 21st-Century Church* (Peabody, MA: Hendrickson Publishers, 2003), 152.

10. Olson, 58.

11. http://www.greeceindex.com/various/greek_love_words.html.

12. http://www.adoptuskids.org/resourcecenter/rrtpackets/ohio.aspx.

13. http://www.forbes.com/2010/02/11/americas-most-miserable-cities-business-beltway-miserable-cities_slide_10.html.

Chapter 4

1. Mark Batterson *Wild Goose Chase* (Sisters, OR: Multnomah Books, 2008), 1. http://www.amazon.com/dp/1590527194/ref=rdr_ext_sb_ti_sims_1#reader_1590527194 (accessed February 18, 2011).

2. Ibid., 4.

Chapter 6

1. http://www.godrules.net/para/2cor/parallel2cor9-7.htm.

2. Warren W. Wiersbe, *The Wiersbe Bible Commentary: The Complete New Testament in One Volume*, second edition (Colorado Springs, CO: David C. Cook, 2007), 497.

Chapter 7

1. Ravi Zacharias, *The Broken Promise* (Colorado Springs, CO: Cook Communications Ministries, 2000). Retold with permission.

2. I am not suggesting that those practicing homosexuality, promiscuity, or any other sin do not need to repent and begin pursuing Christlikeness. I am simply saying that we who are saved should approach them as Jesus approached them—with love, humility, and a passion to bring them into the kingdom.

3. "China," *The Voice of the Martyrs,* Special Issue 2010, 16.

4. "India," Ibid., 17.

5. "Sudan," Ibid., 23.

6. "Richest 2% Own Half the World's Wealth—Study," *The Newsletter of United Nations University and Its International Network of Research and Training Centres/Programmes*, Issue 44, December 2006–February 2007, http://update.unu.edu.

7. Bob Coy, audio recording, "Money Matters part 5," Generous Giving Conference, The Active Word, www.activeword.org.

8. Richard Stearns, quoted in Julia Duin, "Tithing for World in Need," *Washington Times,* March 19, 2009.

9. http://www.unicefusa.org/campaigns/believe-in-zero/ (accessed December 1, 2010).

10. Clint Borgen, "The Top 5 Myths About Global Poverty," http://www.thehuffingtonpost.com, November 11, 2010.

11. http://www.adventconspiracy.org/water/ (accessed December 1, 2010).

12. Claude Rosenberg and Tim Stone, "A New Take on Tithing," *Stanford Social Innovation Review,* Fall 2006.

13. G. Campbell Morgan, quoted by Ravi Zacharias, *Walking from East to West* (Grand Rapids, MI: Zondervan, 2006), 68.

14. Information in this section is retold from Tony Campolo, audio recording, "The Church: God's Instrument for Changing the World," www.tonycampolo.org/sermons and from Tony Campolo, *Let Me Tell You a Story* (Nashville, TN: Thomas Nelson, 2000), 133.

Chapter 8

1. http://www.greenenergyhelpfiles.com/kineticenergy.htm (accessed November 17, 2010).

2. According to e-mail from Gospel for Asia, February 18, 2011.

Chapter 9

1. http://thesaurus.com/opt/Greek-Word-for-Bind.

unleashed

About the Authors

 **Dudley Rutherford** is senior pastor of Shepherd of the Hills Church in Los Angeles. He shares the gospel with about ten thousand people every weekend through twenty different worship services, including four daughter churches and four satellite campuses. He also reaches approximately two million people weekly via radio and television. Dudley is founder of CallonJesus.com, which features his sermons and books, and DreamofDestiny.org—a ministry that fosters racial diversity within church leadership. Dudley is president of the 2011 North American Christian Convention and is an avid sports fan. He lives with his wife and three children in Porter Ranch, California. He blogs at www.dudleyrutherford.blogspot.com and shares regularly on www.twitter.com/pastordudley.

 **Daryl Reed** has ministered in eight churches in six different states across America. Since 2003, he has been lead minister of DC Regional Christian Church, a nondenominational, racially diverse congregation located in metropolitan Washington, DC. Daryl is known for his passion for God and his family, which includes his wife, Charon, and their three teenage sons.

 **Greg Nettle** has been senior pastor of RiverTree Christian Church in northern Ohio for the past twenty years. He travels extensively around the world, specifically caring for children at risk. Greg is the visionary leader of Kingdom Synergy Partnerships, a church planting/

peer-mentoring consortium. He has published numerous articles in *Christian Standard* and blogs regularly at www.gregnettle.com. Greg and his wife live with their two children in Clinton, Ohio.

 **Mike Breaux** is teaching pastor at Heartland Community Church, an innovative ministry in Rockford, Illinois. Through thirty years of ministry, he has been a youth pastor, church planter, and senior pastor, formerly at Southland Christian Church in his hometown of Lexington, Kentucky. Mike is the author of *Making Ripples* and *Identity Theft*. He and his wife have three children.

 **Phil Allen** is pastor of the Vine, the young adult ministry of Shepherd of the Hills Church in Los Angeles, California—a ministry some three thousand miles away from his southern roots of Georgetown, South Carolina. He loves preaching and teaching the Word of God, but even more he loves passing on the relational, organic ministry that Jesus modeled with his twelve disciples.

 **Dave Stone** is senior minister at Southeast Christian Church in Louisville, Kentucky, the fifth largest church in America, where more than twenty-one thousand attend three regional campuses in the Kentuckiana area each weekend. Dave has served on the SCC staff for twenty years and is the author of five books. He and his wife, Beth, have three children. Dave loves an occasional round of golf, competition of any sort, and has a passion for reaching the lost.

unleashed

Jeff Vines is senior pastor of Christ's Church of the Valley in San Dimas, California. Prior to that he spent twenty years on the mission field (in Zimbabwe and New Zealand), planting churches and training leaders. For seven years he was the featured speaker on the weekly television broadcast *Questions for Life,* and frequently debated agnostics and atheists on national radio. He is the author of *Dinner with Skeptics* and has published several articles in *Christian Standard.* Jeff and his wife have two children.

Francis Chan and his wife started Cornerstone Community Church in Simi Valley, California, in 1994, with only thirty people, and he pastored there until August 2010. It is now one of the largest churches in Ventura County. Francis is also founder and chancellor of Eternity Bible College and is an internationally sought-after conference speaker. He is a best-selling author of two books, *Crazy Love* and *Forgotten God.* He blogs at www.francischan.org. Francis and his wife have four children.

Jeff Walling is senior minister of Providence Road Church of Christ, in Charlotte, North Carolina. His passionate style and dramatic delivery have made him a sought-after speaker. He lectures to tens of thousands annually at Christian universities, evangelism seminars, and conferences worldwide. Jeff has written *Daring to Dance with God, Hugs for Grads,* and *Until I Return.* A California native, he and his wife, Cathryn, have called Charlotte home for fourteen years . . . but they still miss Disneyland.

Keep turning the world upside down with these great resources!